Brand Naming

Brand Naming

The Complete Guide to Creating a Name
for Your Company, Product, or Service

Rob Meyerson

BUSINESS EXPERT PRESS

Leader in applied, concise business books

First published in 2021 by
Business Expert Press, LLC
222 East 46th Street, New York, NY 10017
www.businessexpertpress.com

ISBN-13: 978-1-63742-155-0 (paperback)
ISBN-13: 978-1-63742-156-7 (e-book)

Business Expert Press Marketing Collection

Collection ISSN: 2169-3978 (print)
Collection ISSN: 2169-3986 (electronic)

First edition: 2021

10 9 8 7 6 5 4 3 2 1

For Mom and Dad.
Thanks for always supporting me and never charging
for your editing services.

Description

You don't have a brand—whether it's for a company or a product—until you have a name. The name is one of the first, longest lasting, and most important decisions in defining the identity of a company, product, or service. But set against a tidal wave of trademark applications, mortifying mistranslations, and disappearing dot-com availability, you won't find a good name by dumping out the Scrabble tiles or running an all-employee contest.

In fact, the challenges of naming are so great they've given rise to a new breed of branding expert: the professional namer. *Brand Naming* details best-practice methodologies, tactics, and advice from the world of professional naming, shared by Rob Meyerson, a brand strategist and namer who's named start-ups, nonprofits, and products of the Fortune 500. You'll learn what makes a good (and bad) name, the step-by-step process namers use, and how to generate hundreds of ideas before whittling the list down to a finalist.

The most complete and detailed book about naming your brand, *Brand Naming* also includes insider anecdotes (what Phil Knight said when he first heard *Nike*), tired trends (start-ups with names ending in *ly*), busted myths (Chevy Nova sold just fine in Mexico), and brand origin stories (the surprising truth behind *Häagen-Dazs*). And through interviews with over a dozen other namers, Meyerson has amassed a treasure trove of resources, references, templates, and tools to help you dive deeper into the art and science of naming. So, whether you need a great name for a new company or product or just want to learn the secrets of professional word nerds, put down the thesaurus—not to mention Scrabble—and pick up *Brand Naming*.

Keywords

branding; marketing; brand naming; company naming; business naming; product naming; brand names; how to name a company; how to name a product; brand identity; brand strategy; brand consulting; small business marketing; start-up marketing; marketing for entrepreneurs; brand management; brand marketing; verbal identity; nomenclature; product management; product marketing; entrepreneurs; start-ups; small business

As soon as you label a concept, you change how people perceive it.
—Adam Alter, "The Power of Names,"
The New Yorker

Contents

Testimonials

"A brand name is the number-one touchpoint a product or company will ever own. And now, thanks to the generous clarity of Rob Meyerson, there's a book about it. Get this onto your shelf."—**Marty Neumeier, author,** *The Brand Gap*

"This is the bible for brand namers. Brand Naming *is the resource that all branding professionals need to have at their fingertips. Armed with the rigorous process, illuminating examples, and thorough list of resources in this book, you will be able to create a valuable brand name with confidence."* —**Denise Lee Yohn, brand leadership expert; author,** *What Great Brands Do*

"This book is breathtakingly complete in its coverage of naming. It's also entertaining—full of fun naming anecdotes. A brand name can dramatically affect the success of a new brand and can enable or constrain future strategies. You need to read this book to get your brand name right."—**David Aaker, Vice Chairman, Prophet; author,** *Aaker on Branding*

"Rob Meyerson has written a must-read: Brand Naming: The Complete Guide to Creating a Name for Your Company, Product, or Service, *which is the most complete and detailed book about naming. Read this book and you will be learning from one of the best."*—**Martin Lindstrom, Founder and Chairman of Lindstrom Company; author,** *Brand Sense* **and** *Buyology*

"Naming is one of the most critical steps in building a winning brand, and it's hands down the most challenging. This book provides an incredibly thoughtful, thorough, and actionable resource, with invaluable guidance on what matters most when choosing a name, and what doesn't matter at all. It's a must read for agencies and entrepreneurs alike!"—**Emily Heyward, Co-Founder, Red Antler; author,** *Obsessed*

"Naming is a beast, and this book slays. My brand strategy book collection was missing this key resource. Set next to Aaker on brand architecture and Neumeier on brand positioning, Meyerson delivers the keystone guide to brand naming. This permanent desk resource is perfect for the entrepreneur or the brand classroom. Don't name anything without it."—**Sasha Strauss, Founder and CEO, Innovation Protocol; Faculty, USC Marshall, UCLA Anderson, and UC Irvine Merage Graduate Business Schools**

Foreword

If brands have become the global currency of success, then brand names must be the essential units of that currency. A brand does not exist without a name.

The name of your company or product will be spoken, written, and shared countless times across myriad digital and physical touchpoints in perpetuity. It is the Energizer Bunny of brand assets. The best names withstand massive disruptions in technology, adapt to shifts in the global economy and customer preferences, and resonate as the brand of choice.

Naming is not for the faint of heart. It is a complex, creative, and iterative process that integrates expertise in brand strategy, marketing, research, linguistics, intellectual property law, and—as Rob Meyerson underscores—human psychology. Names need to be judged against positioning goals, performance criteria, and availability. Everyone wants to fall in love, so agreement is difficult, because legal choices are limited and deadlines loom. The process takes patience, and the final decision takes fortitude—the courage to make a commitment to the future.

Brand Naming is an essential resource for your branding team. It's the most comprehensive naming book that I know of—Rob doesn't prescribe a single "best" way but shares multiple approaches and methodologies from a variety of experts. His book prepares you to succeed by setting out a clear process for naming—meticulously deconstructing every step, from writing a naming brief, to exploring *lexical caves*, to preparing you to mitigate resistance and build consensus with key decision makers. Even with this level of detail, *Brand Naming* is an easy and engaging read, impeccably researched and thoughtfully constructed. If you have listened to his podcast, *How Brands Are Built,* you have heard firsthand what an effective communicator Rob is. He has that rare talent of being able to write as clearly as he speaks.

Rob has occupied every seat at the naming table, from start-ups to mature, multinational, public companies. He's led naming projects at world-renowned brand consultancies, generated thousands of name ideas for hundreds of projects, and served as a one-man naming department for boutique agencies. He has lived and worked in Silicon Valley, Shanghai, and Southeast Asia, and understands the importance of cultural insights. As Global Head of Naming at HP, he led a team of naming and brand strategists, hired and managed top-tier naming firms, and helped make sense of the million-plus "named things" at a massive, complex organization.

Are you the head of marketing about to hire a naming consultant, looking to understand more about the discipline and what it will take? Are you a brand consultant hoping to grow your strategy and naming business? Or maybe your CEO has given you the daunting task of leading an in-house naming initiative. Regardless of your situation, your sector, or the size of your organization, finding a name for a new company, product, or service presents a formidable challenge. It's emotional. It's political. It's important. Before you embark on naming or renaming your company or product, invest in this book. The ROI is off the charts.

—Alina Wheeler
Author, *Designing Brand Identity:*
An Essential Guide for the Whole Branding Team
Philadelphia, 2021

Acknowledgments

For graciously sharing their knowledge on the *How Brands Are Built* podcast and for agreeing to let me quote them throughout this book, thank you to all my season-one guests: Eli Altman, Jonathan Bell, Clive Chafer, Shannon DeJong, Scott Milano, Amanda C. Peterson, Steven Price, Anthony Shore, and Laurel Sutton. I'm lucky to have had them on the show and even luckier to call many of them mentors, colleagues, and friends. Thanks also to every other podcast guest, including naming experts (and authors!) Brad Flowers and Jeremy Miller.

Alan Brew and Rob Goodman took hours out of their busy lives to read and provide notes on previous drafts of this book. Perry Gattegno of Litwin Kach reviewed and suggested edits to the article on which the trademark prescreening chapter is based. The final product is richer, smarter, and clearer thanks to their feedback.

When I told Fabian Geyrhalter, Marty Neumeier, and Alina Wheeler of my plans to write this book, they each jumped at the opportunity to share their experiences and insights on writing and getting published. If you haven't already read their respective books on brand strategy and identity, you're missing out.

Scott Isenberg, Dr. Naresh Malhotra, Rob Zwettler, and everyone at Business Expert Press—thank you for your confidence in this book.

Thanks also to every client, colleague, and partner I've had the pleasure of working with, many of whom taught me valuable lessons about branding and naming.

Lastly, thanks most of all to my family. To Mom, Dad, and Adam for ensuring I was raised in a home full of intellectual curiosity and good words. To the kids for giving me time to write this book between rounds of hide-and-seek. And to Ashley for the never-ending honeymoon phase. Love you.

Introduction

A few years ago, Ron Marshall, owner of a small marketing firm in Springfield, Missouri, decided to count how many brands and ads he saw in a single day. That morning, he woke up to his *Sony* alarm clock, got dressed and put on his *Nike* shoes, and drank a cup of *Folgers* coffee. After making note of those brands—and 484 others—he gave up counting. That was before he'd finished breakfast.

By most estimates, we see thousands of brand names every day. The brands may vary in different parts of the world—Li-Ning instead of Nike, say, or Nescafé instead of Folgers—but the pattern is the same. Next time you open your medicine cabinet or kitchen pantry, try counting, and you'll start to get an idea of just how inundated we all are.

And yet, most of us rarely think twice about the origins or meanings of brand names. What (or who) is a Sony, Folgers, or Li-Ning? How and why were these names selected? What do they mean? Does it even matter?

For those of us who work in the fields of naming, branding, and—more broadly—marketing, it can matter a great deal. According to Michael Eisner, former CEO of Disney, brands are "enriched or undermined cumulatively over time, the product[s] of a thousand small gestures." A name is one such gesture—it matters because it's one of many opportunities to convey the important ideas, attributes, or characteristics that make up a brand. And brands, when built and conveyed well, are good for business.

Granted, a great brand name can't save a failing company or product. For example, Brandless, an ironically named brand of three-dollar food and pantry items sold online, went out of business after less than three years despite a name that many professionals considered first-rate. Conversely, many business success stories begin with dubious naming decisions. Mondelēz, whose name was mostly panned by branding experts upon its launch in 2012, has nearly doubled its stock price since then. But because brands are built "cumulatively over time," as Eisner teaches us, every detail can make a difference—from the color of a logo to the spelling of a name. If you're aiming to build a strong brand, start with a strong brand name.

***

I've been a professional brand namer for over 15 years. Yes, it's a real job. Of course, many people come up with brand names on occasion—copywriters, product managers, start-up founders, and entrepreneurs—but only professional namers get paid to run a full naming process from start to finish. And only namers will take on a stand-alone project with just one deliverable: a strategically optimal, legally available, linguistically viable, client-approved brand name.

I worked on my first naming assignment at Interbrand in 2005. The head of naming at Interbrand's San Francisco office back then was Andrzej Olszewski. (He was fond of saying, "Don't worry, I didn't pick my own name.") Even though I wasn't on Andrzej's team, he kindly sent me a naming brief when he needed additional ideas for an especially vexing assignment. The brief requested ideas that evoked flexibility. I suggested *Asana*, a word meaning *yoga pose*.[1] Andrzej liked it. I was hooked.

I've always been a bit of a word nerd. As a kid, my favorite game at family get-togethers was Balderdash, in which players invent definitions for obscure words such as *perwitsky* and *pilcrow*.[2] In college, I attended a presentation by Will Shortz, crossword puzzle editor for *The New York Times*. (I also studied phonetics, worked in a psycholinguistics lab, and majored in cognitive science with a concentration in linguistics.) After reading a book about the competitive world of Scrabble,[3] I dragged a friend to a meeting of the San Francisco Scrabble Club. And a few of my 55-word *flash fiction* stories have been published as winners of an annual contest. But naming represented a new and unique way of flexing my creative, lexical, and lateral thinking muscles. And I could get paid to do it!

---

[1] Sadly, the client did not pick my name idea. Three years later, *Asana*, the billion-dollar project management software company, was founded.

[2] According to the game, a perwitsky is "a European skunk whose fur is used to make paintbrushes" and *pilcrow* means "very hairy." *Balderdash*, meanwhile, is a real word meaning *nonsense*.

[3] *Word Freak* by Stefan Fatsis. (It's fantastic.)

After Interbrand, I was eager for more opportunities to do naming work, so I started moonlighting—a freelance namer for hire. In the years since, I've worked on naming projects for just about every naming and branding firm out there. I've worked with clients such as Activision, AT&T, Disney, GE, Intel, and Microsoft. I've named start-ups, non-profits, and the products and services of the Fortune 500. I've named a Malaysian resort, a Chinese state-owned enterprise, and something in Romania called a *pizza cone*. More recently, I was Global Head of Naming at Hewlett-Packard (HP[4]). There, I led a small team tasked with triaging an onslaught of inbound naming requests—over a hundred at any given time—sent to us by any of 300,000 employees around the world.

Along the way, I learned that coming up with a list of brilliant name ideas will only get you so far. Getting a group of people to agree on a single word that's meant to convey the essence of a company or product requires more than creativity—it takes adherence to a proven naming process. By working with naming veterans,[5] listening to feedback from clients, and suffering through a fair bit of trial and error, I've picked up a litany of tips, tools, and techniques for getting to a great name. In short, I've learned the best practices used by professional namers to run a successful naming project—start to finish. And that's what I've documented in this book.

In Part I, you'll learn the **Background and basics** of brand naming, including what makes a good (or bad) brand name, types of names, and the basic naming process. In Part II, you'll see how namers generate **Hundreds of ideas** for each project, starting with a naming brief and leaving no stone unturned. And in Part III, you'll get step-by-step instructions on the process for **Narrowing down to one** final name, including preliminary trademark screening and linguistic checks, delivering a solid naming presentation, and, finally, launching the new name. At the end of

---

[4] A month or two after I joined, the CEO announced that HP would split into two companies: HP Inc. and Hewlett Packard Enterprise. HP Inc. retained the old company's brand identity, including the blue logo and the name *HP*. Technically, the company named *Hewlett-Packard* no longer exists.

[5] Many of whom I've also interviewed on my podcast, *How Brands Are Built*.

the book, in Part IV, you'll find a treasure trove of **Resources**—reference materials, websites, templates, and more.

My goal for *Brand Naming* is simple: to create the most comprehensive, substantive, and well-informed guide to brand naming. Whether you're a marketing professional or an entrepreneur, naming your company or hiring an agency to name something for you, you'll benefit from the ideas, processes, tips, and resources herein. By reading this book, you'll discover what took me years to fully understand: How to consistently create great names for companies, products, and services.

PART I

Background and Basics

I read in a book once that a rose by any other name would smell as sweet, but I've never been able to believe it. I don't believe a rose would be as nice if it was called a thistle or a skunk cabbage.

—L.M. Montgomery, *Anne of Green Gables*

CHAPTER 1

How Brand Naming Works

Key Ideas

- Brand names can shift perceptions and influence business outcomes.
- Naming is important because language is powerful, naming is hard, and a good brand name is a good investment.
- Good brand names strike a balance between strategic, creative, and technical qualities.

Much to the annoyance of every namer I know, it seems there's an unwritten rule that all articles and blog posts about brand naming must start with the same familiar quotation:[1]

> *What's in a name? That which we call a rose*
> *By any other name would smell as sweet*
> —William Shakespeare, *Romeo and Juliet*

Shakespeare's Juliet was partly right, of course: changing something's name won't change its underlying properties. A rose by any other name *would* smell just as sweet. Or, at least, it would emit the same odor molecules.

But names, like any other words we use to describe and label things, affect our perceptions. And perceptions—not just odor molecules—determine how we experience the world around us. That's why Antarctic toothfish by another name, *Chilean sea bass*, sells better.

---

[1] In fact, "What's in a name?" is often used as the title of the article. If not that, it's almost always "The name game." If you're writing about naming, please use something else.

When it comes to brand names—words used to identify companies, products, or services—shifts in perception can lead to shifts in business outcomes. Just as a CEO's confidence can influence an investor's decision to buy or sell, a brand name (and, more broadly, a brand identity) can influence a customer's decision to buy or not buy or a recruit's decision to take a job or pass. In business, as in life, perceptions matter.

But just how important *is* naming? After all, most brand names are just a handful of letters, and some of the most successful companies and products don't seem to have had much thought put into theirs. *General Motors* and *BestBuy* are about as dry as you can get. *Snickers* and *Bluetooth* don't seem to have any relevant meaning. *Yahoo* sounds irresponsible, and *Diesel* sounds smelly and bad for the planet.[2] If brands with these names succeeded, couldn't *anything* work as a brand name?

Maybe. Unfortunately, names join many other marketing elements in suffering from an *attribution problem.* If a brand does well, how much of that success is attributable to a great brand name? If a company fails, to what degree could that failure be attributed to a terrible name? Because every brand is the sum of its integrated parts, we can't easily assign value to a good or bad name in isolation. Nevertheless, it seems wise to steer clear of the branding equivalent of *toothfish* if we can avoid it. Better to have a name that opens doors than one that opens a can of worms.

Because of the ambiguity surrounding the value of finding the right brand name, a namer's first task is often to explain the importance of naming (and, sometimes, justify the price tag for a naming process). When faced with this challenge, I make the following three points: language is powerful, naming is hard, and a good name is a good investment.

Language Is Powerful

Steven Pinker, noted psychologist and linguist, describes language as "one of the wonders of the natural world," a uniquely human ability to "shape events in each other's brains with exquisite precision."[3] And anyone who's

---

[2] For the record, I'm not necessarily saying these are bad brand names. *Diesel*, in fact, is great. *Yahoo*, not so much.

[3] S. Pinker. 2007. *The Language Instinct* (New York: HarperCollins).

been moved by a novel, inspired by a passionate speech, or haunted by heartfelt song lyrics knows the power of language to not only describe events but to spur emotion.

The effect of language has also been studied empirically. In 1974, two psychologists sought to understand how language affects perceptions.[4] They showed videos of car accidents to students and asked them to estimate how fast the cars were moving at the moment of impact. But for each group of students, the researchers phrased their question slightly differently. Participants who were asked, "About how fast were the cars going when they *smashed* each other?" reported the cars moving at over 40 miles per hour. Those asked how fast the cars were moving when they *contacted* each other estimated speeds closer to 30. By changing a verb, and nothing else, the psychologists were able to alter participants' perceptions and memories of the accidents.

The food industry has demonstrated an understanding of the power of language to influence consumers—not only with Chilean sea bass, but with products ranging from canola oil—née *rapeseed oil*—to dried plums—the fruit formerly known as *prunes*. Politicians, too, have used (and abused) language to great effect,[5] framing and reframing debates through terms like *pro-life, death tax,* and *gun safety.*[6]

The brand name is a prime opportunity for businesspeople to harness the power of language to convey meaning and inspire emotion.

Naming Is Hard

A lot can go wrong without a proper naming process. Just ask the people behind naming missteps like Boaty McBoatface (see Chapter 5) or Consignia and Tronc (see details below in *What Makes a Bad Brand Name?*).

---

[4] E.F. Loftus, and J.C. Palmer. 1974. "Reconstruction of Automobile Destruction: An Example of the Interaction Between Language and Memory." *Journal of Verbal Learning and Verbal Behavior* 13, no. 5, pp. 585–589.

[5] D. Aaker. August 02, 2012. "What Your Brand Can Learn From Political Rhetoric," *Harvard Business Review.* https://hbr.org/2012/08/what-your-brand-can-learn-from

[6] As opposed to *anti-abortion, estate tax,* and *gun control,* respectively.

In fact, some of the best clients for naming and branding agencies are the ones who've already tried to do it themselves—they call, exasperated, and complain that no one on the team can agree on anything or all the good names are already taken.

That's because, unlike coming up with a cute name for a pet, naming in a business context means aligning on objectives, considering legal and cultural implications, and driving consensus around something that—despite efforts to inject objectivity into the process—can ultimately feel like a gut call. In the words of a 2011 article in *The New Yorker*, the process "can be arduous, and often comes down to a combination of instinct, abstract reasoning, and the client's idiosyncratic demands."[7]

And that's all *before* the name has launched. As we'll explore further at the end of this chapter and at other points throughout the book, ill-considered brand names that make it out into the wild can result in product recalls, wasted money, and legal problems—not to mention embarrassment.

A Good Name Is a Good Investment

The contemporary meaning of *brand* is a bit hard to pin down. Definitions range from pithy—"what people say about you when you're not in the room"[8]—to straightlaced—"a name, term, design, symbol, or any other feature that identifies one seller's good or service as distinct from those of other sellers."[9] Far less debated is the idea that a strong brand—one that's instantly recognizable, emotionally resonant, and consistently expressed—can help a business meet its goals, from building awareness to increasing market share.[10]

---

[7] J. Colapinto. September 26, 2011. "Famous Names." *New Yorker*. https://www .newyorker.com/magazine/2011/10/03/famous-names

[8] Commonly attributed to Jeff Bezos, although it's tough to find evidence he actually said this.

[9] "Common Language Marketing Dictionary." n.d. *Brand.* https://marketing-dictionary.org/b/brand/ (accessed May 24, 2021).

[10] B. Sharp. 2010. *How Brands Grow.* Melbourne: Oxford University Press.

If you've come around to the idea that branding will help your business achieve its goals, the importance of brand names is hard to deny. Of all the marketing decisions brand owners make, the name is likely to last the longest. Through all the ad campaigns, website refreshes, and logo redesigns, the brand name remains.

And compared to those other marketing activities, a good name is an inexpensive way to grab attention in a crowded marketplace. Take an example from the auto industry: In a sea of names that are drab, meaningless, or both—*Volkswagen, Toyota, Ford, GM*—a name like *Tesla* stands out, sparks curiosity, and instantly conveys more meaning than most of its competitors' multimillion-dollar ad campaigns. As mentioned above, it's impossible to know whether Tesla Motors could have been equally successful with another name. But Elon Musk, Tesla's CEO, saw the name's potential; he had the company spend $75,000 to acquire the rights to use it.[11]

What Makes a Good Brand Name?

In early 2021, Alan Brew, founding partner at BrandingBusiness, ran an informal survey among professional namers. In an e-mail titled "I wish I'd thought of that," he made one, simple request: "Nominate a brand name (consumer or corporate) from any era that you really like and admire, with a sentence or two elaborating on why you like it."

Replies included names like *Twitter, Wawa, Macintosh,* and *DieHard* (the car batteries, not the movie). However, I was more interested in the explanations these namers gave for their choices. They selected names that, by their estimation, "broke free of ... naming conventions," "capture[d] the spirit of [the] product," had "staying power," and were "unexpected," "extendable," or "hard to forget."

Whether you're asking a naming pro or not, you'll find no shortage of strong opinions on what makes a good brand name. Leading naming firms like A Hundred Monkeys and Catchword each present their own lists of the half-dozen qualities they feel define effective brand names. You'll find similar lists in famous branding books, from Marty Neumeier's

---

[11] E. Musk. 2018. Interview with Lesley Stahl. *60 Minutes*, December 09, CBS.

The Brand Gap to Alina Wheeler's *Designing Brand Identity.* Search online, and you'll find countless articles by marketers or entrepreneurs—with varying degrees of naming expertise—on the three, five, or seven things every great brand name must do.

These lists can be useful, but they're oversimplifications. What makes a name good depends on the context and underlying strategy. Brand names don't exist in a vacuum. Exciting, edgy names are great, but in a market full of names shouting "look at me!" an understated name might be the best way to stand out. Consider the bottled water industry, where names range from evocative and self-important—*Fiji* and *Pure Life*—to downright strange—*Dasani* and *Fred.* In this context, a straight-shooting name like *Smartwater* is notable for its refreshing simplicity—a good description of how I like my water, coincidentally.[12]

The strategy behind the name, including basic information like what's being named, what the name is meant to express, and what names competitors are using, will dictate which ideas are best—not in abstract, absolute terms, but specifically with respect to the project at hand. Lists of supposed must haves for brand names, then, are not the hard-and-fast rules their authors make them out to be—think of them instead as general guidelines to bear in mind when comparing otherwise similar names. These factors that contribute to the strength of a name fall into three areas: strategic, creative, and technical.

Strategic Qualities of Good Names

By *strategic*, I mean the name should be rooted in brand strategy and aligned with business strategy. That might mean making sure the name expresses a particular idea, evokes a specific emotion, or uses or avoids certain words. Stick to the strategy, and you should be left with ideas that meet some or all three of the following criteria, each of which can help ensure a strategically successful brand name:

---

[12] This logic can also be applied to a book title. Even when the book in question is about brand naming.

- Meaningful: conveys the intended message and evokes the right feelings; resonates with the intended audience
- Adaptable: able to stretch to accommodate foreseeable changes in the brand or business; can serve as a springboard to create a unique *brand language* around the name[13]
- Distinctive: stands out when compared with names of competitors or peers

Creative Qualities of Good Names

Creativity is subjective, and the criteria below are more open to interpretation than those in the strategic and technical areas. But even when making subjective judgments about a name, it's useful to break up big, nebulous questions like *Is it creative?* into smaller, more manageable questions. When pitting name candidates against each other, consider the following creative factors:

- Memorable: catches attention and sticks in the mind due to distinctiveness, brevity, emotional resonance, or structural features of the name like alliteration, assonance (consistent vowel sounds), or rhyming
- Sounds good: sonically pleasing or fun to say
- Looks good: composed of letters that are visually appealing when written out (or when designed as a wordmark)[14]

Technical Qualities of Good Names

Lastly, every successful brand name must jump through a few technical hoops. This is a big part of what makes naming so difficult. Unfortunately, any name that seems perfect to you will likely have seemed perfect to others, too—making it difficult for you to use the name without facing

---

[13] As the name *Twitter* has—whether encouraged by the company or inspired by users—with words like *Tweet*, *Tweeps*, and *Twittersphere*.

[14] All or part of a logo featuring the brand name written in a distinctive, standardized typographical treatment.

legal repercussions. Names can also suffer from linguistic, spelling, or pronunciation challenges. Screen name ideas to see whether they're likely to succeed in navigating the following technical hoops:

- Legally available: unlikely to result in legal problems arising from similarity to another name used for similar goods and services
- Linguistically viable: avoids inappropriate meanings, connotations, associations, and pronunciation challenges in relevant languages and cultures
- Easy to spell and pronounce: unlikely to cause confusion due to similarity to other words[15] or strange, incorrect, or overly difficult spelling; unambiguous pronunciation that rolls off the tongue

Note that the nine criteria shown in Figure 1.1 are not interdependent—some overlap significantly with others. Names that are distinctive are more likely to be memorable. Names that are hard to pronounce might also suffer from linguistic challenges or a lack of memorability. A name that's easy to pronounce, on the other hand, is more likely to sound good. (Although *crud* is easy to pronounce.)

Nor are these criteria equally important, necessarily. A lack of legal availability tends to trump other factors; if someone's already using the name for something similar, who cares how sonically pleasing it is? And project-specific strategy can drive the relative importance of criteria, too—whether ease of pronunciation in other countries is paramount or irrelevant, for example, or the degree to which a name is likely to need to stretch beyond its original meaning. All three areas—strategic, creative, and technical—and the criteria within them must be brought into the right balance for each project.

---

[15] For example, a name like *Hone* could easily be mistaken for *Home*, requiring a constant *n-as-in-Nancy* clarification.

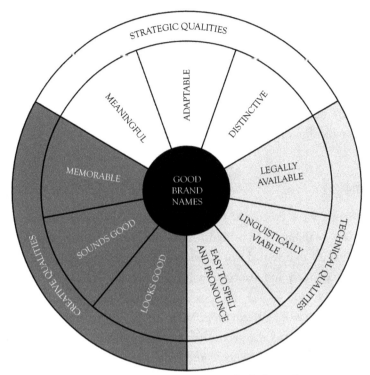

Figure 1.1 Good brand names strike the right balance between a range of strategic, creative, and technical criteria

A Few Good Names

To further explore the factors that contribute to the strength of a name, let's take a look at a few of the best brand names out there:

Apple

Often cited as a brilliant company name, *Apple* apparently came to Steve Jobs when he "had just come back from the apple farm."[16] He chose it

---

[16] In a 2011 *Seattle Times* article, Jobs's business partner Steve Wozniak pointed out that the apple farm "was actually a commune." (R. Metz, October 06, 2011. "Apple co-founder Wozniak recalls a friend in Jobs." *Seattle Times*. https://www .seattletimes.com/business/apple-co-founder-wozniak-recalls-a-friend-in-jobs).

because it "sounded fun, spirited, and not intimidating."[17] It's light on relevant meaning—although some say it's meant to suggest simplicity—but it more than compensates with distinctiveness, standing out against its 1970s and 1980s-era contemporaries like Commodore, Microsoft, and IBM.[18] Furthermore, it's adaptable (as evidenced by Apple-branded products ranging from a streaming video service to a digital stylus), memorable, fun to say, and easy to spell.

Swiffer

This name for a Procter & Gamble mop was created by Lexicon, the Bay Area branding firm behind names like *Pentium, Sonos,* and *Zima.* Although it's an invented word, *Swiffer* still carries some meaning thanks to onomatopoeia and associations between *sw* and everyday words like *sweep, swish,* and *swoosh.* It's also a distinctive name when compared with competitors like ReadyMop, Turbo Mop, and Snap Mop (notice a trend?). Add the fact that, according to National Public Radio, it's "easy to pronounce in any language,"[19] and *Swiffer* seems to meet all the criteria outlined above.

Kodak

Dating back to 1888, *Kodak* is a meaningless, made-up word. Founder George Eastman liked the "strong, incisive" nature of the letter *k,* and created—as described in a 1920 Kodak ad[20] (Figure 1.2)—a "short and euphonious" name that was "likely to stick in the public mind" and "meet

---

[17] W. Isaacson. 2011. *Steve Jobs* (London: Simon & Schuster).

[18] Maybe that's why Jobs and Wozniak rejected other ideas like *Executex* and *Matrix Computers,* which would have blended in.

[19] E. Blair. May 13, 2011. "With Billions at Stake, Firms Play Name That Mop." *NPR.* https://www.npr.org/2011/05/13/136024080/with-billions-at-stake-firms-play-name-that-mop

[20] Eastman Kodak Company. February 1920. "The History of a Word." Advertisement. *Kodakery,* The GenWeb of Monroe County, Kodak Collection. https://mcnygenealogy.com/book/kodak/kodakery-1920-02.pdf

The History of a Word

THE trade-mark "Kodak" was first applied, in 1888, to a camera manufactured by us and intended for amateur use. It had no "derivation." It was simply invented—made up from letters of the alphabet to meet our trade-mark requirements.

It was short and euphonious and likely to stick in the public mind, and therefore seemed to us to be admirably adapted to use in exploiting our new product.

It was, of course, immediately registered, and so is ours, both by such registration and by common law. Its first application was to the Kodak Camera. Since then we have applied it to other goods of our manufacture, as, for instance, Kodak Tripods, Kodak Portrait Attachments, Kodak Film, Kodak Film Tanks and Kodak Amateur Printers.

The name "Kodak" does not mean that these goods must be used in connection with a Kodak Camera, for as a matter of fact any of them may be used with other apparatus or goods. It simply means that they originated with, and are manufactured by, the Eastman Kodak Company.

"Kodak" being our registered and common law trade-mark can not be rightly applied except to goods of our manufacture.

If you ask at the store for a Kodak Camera or Kodak Film, or other Kodak goods and are handed something not of our manufacture, you are not getting what you specified, which is obviously unfair both to you and to us.

If it isn't an Eastman, it isn't a Kodak.

Eastman Kodak Company

Rochester, New York, *The Kodak City.*

Figure 1.2 *Full-page Kodak ad from 1920*

our trade-mark requirements." The same ad notes that *Kodak* has been used for cameras and "other goods of our manufacture," demonstrating the ability of the name to stretch beyond its original use. So, while it has no inherent meaning, the name was chosen because it sounds good, it's memorable, it was legally available, and it's adaptable. Well done, Mr. Eastman.

Honestly, it's impossible to fairly judge a brand name—or just about any other creative work, for that matter—from the outside looking in. We weren't in the room when these names were created, and we have no direct access to the strategic thinking (or lack thereof) that went into them. And without some serious digging, we'll never know what uphill battles these brands may have faced from a legal or linguistic standpoint. Still, great names like *Apple, Swiffer,* and *Kodak* show how successfully meeting many—but not necessarily all—of the criteria outlined above can help ensure a good brand name.

What Makes a Bad Brand Name?

Everyone loves a good marketing horror story, from unintentionally suggestive logos to hilariously tone-deaf advertisements. Brand names are no different, and while it's tough to find a name that everyone likes, some names are almost universally hated from day one.

What is it about some names that causes them to draw such ire from the media and the public? The obvious way to understand what makes a bad name is to flip the characteristics of a good name. Some names, like *International House of Pancakes (IHOP)*, aren't adaptive and can't stretch beyond their initial meaning. When the chain wanted to remind customers that they sell burgers in addition to breakfast food, the name became a limitation, leading to a much-derided campaign teasing a new brand name: *IHOb.* Other names are hard to pronounce, like *Hyundai.* The automaker even ran a how-to-pronounce-our-name ad during the Super Bowl in 2009. (If you're wondering, it rhymes with *Sunday.*) And still other names run into trademark or linguistic challenges.

But brand names have other opportunities to fail, too. Even those that avoid these obvious, opposite-of-good problems can still fall flat in at least three additional ways:

1. Overexplained turducken names[21]

Over time, successful names are imbued with many meanings, positive associations glomming onto them like dust onto an electrostatic Swiffer cloth. But a new name, as namers are fond of reminding their clients, can only say one or two things.

Mondelēz, the company behind Oreo, Cadbury, and other snack brands, is a clumsy mashup of *monde*, Latin for *world*, and *delēz*, meant to convey deliciousness. Together, the parts of the name supposedly evoke *delicious world*. And then there's that line over the *e* (a *macron*), which the company hopes will remind you to say *mohn-dah-LEEZ*.

Like a Double Stuf Oreo, the final name is overfilled. Trying to pack too much meaning into a name, especially by claiming each syllable represents a discrete idea, can result in a Frankenstein's monster—hideous and, most likely, doomed.

2. Inside jokes and secret codes

Names don't work when they rely too heavily on esoteric information or nonpublic knowledge. Amateur namers will often pull words from their own areas of expertise—which is great, but can go too far. Just because *you* know that myelin is a substance that insulates nerve cells, don't assume anyone will think *Myelin* is a clever name for a home insulation company. Avoid obscure references, irrelevant jargon, and too-cute metaphors when creating names.

3. Trendchasers

Since at least the early 1900s, every era has come with its share of brand naming trends, from names ending in *o*—like *Jell-O* in 1897, *Brasso* in 1905, *Brillo* in 1913, and *Mentos* in 1932—to today's seemingly never-ending list of names ending in *ly*—*Bitly*, *Insightly*, and *Optimizely*, just to name a few.[22] Unless you want a soundalike name that's timestamped with the era in which it was created, steer clear of trends.

---

[21] A turducken, also known as a three-bird roast, is a chicken stuffed into a duck stuffed into a turkey.

[22] For years, naming expert Nancy Friedman has been keeping a Pinterest board of names ending in *ly*. So far, she's collected over 300.

A Few Bad Names

Just as we used *Apple, Swiffer,* and *Kodak* to highlight the factors that can help strengthen a name, let's do a postmortem on some of the all-time worst brand names to see what we can learn about what did them in:

Consignia

Widely considered one of the worst naming fails of all time, *Consignia* was the new name for Britain's Post Office Group, launched in 2001. Post office leadership described the name as "modern, meaningful, and entirely appropriate." The British public disagreed.

Chief among the name's sins is the fact that it just sounds wrong—like a "Roman general" or "tummy bug," according to one BBC reporter.[23] The portmanteau of *consign* and *insignia* comes across as an awkward attempt to stuff too many ideas into four syllables—a pointless effort, given neither word has much relevant meaning to begin with. (According to the post office, *consign* worked because it means *to entrust to the care of,* and *insignia* gave rise to "this kind of royalty-ish thing in the back of one's mind.") A mere 15 months after its announcement, *Consignia* was returned to sender, replaced by *Royal Mail Group.*[24]

Qwikster

Remember Qwikster? If not, that's probably because it never amounted to much more than a regrettable press release. In 2011, Netflix announced it

---

[23] M. Verdin. March 13, 2002. "Consignia: Nine Letters That Spelled Fiasco," *BBC News.* http://news.bbc.co.uk/2/hi/business/2002480.stm

[24] In fairness, Consignia's swift demise may have had as much to do with external factors and a poorly planned launch as with problems inherent to the name. The rebrand coincided with dismal financial performance and layoffs at the post office. Even worse, the name change was never clearly explained to the British citizenry, the tabloid press playing no small part in stirring up and extending the controversy. When new Post Office Group leadership arrived in the midst of public outcry, they saw an opportunity to win some goodwill by reversing the *Consignia* decision.

would be splitting its business in two: Netflix would continue to provide streaming services, while a new subsidiary, Qwikster, would take over the DVD-by-mail business. A month later, Netflix reversed the decision after tens of thousands of customers expressed their outrage over the idea of having to create two separate accounts.

The business strategy behind this move was questionable, at best, but the name made things even worse. First off, it's hard to remember which wrong spelling is right: Qwickster? Quikster? Quickster? Secondly, this name combines a convenience store naming trope (e.g., QuikStop, Kwik Trip) with an early-2000s naming trend (a la Napster and Friendster). And finally, the only meaning the name conveys is speed, which doesn't make a lot of sense given that, compared to streaming video, waiting for a DVD via snail mail is the slower option.

Tronc

"Tronc to change name back to Tribune Publishing after years of ridicule," read one headline in June 2018.[25] Short for *Tribune Online Content*, *Tronc* had a two-year stint as the name of Tribune Publishing, a Chicago-based newspaper publisher. Like *Consignia*, the biggest problem with this name is that it sounds like something unpleasant. In the words of Nancy Friedman, a naming expert who blogs as Fritinancy, it's "silly at best, ugly at worst, a rhyming cousin of honk, zonk, bonk, and honky-tonk."[26] It also *looks* bad (a garish, all-lowercase logo didn't help). And, as many abbreviations do, it takes a meaningful, albeit jargon-laden, phrase—Tribune Online Content—and strips it of meaning for anyone other than the few who remember what it stands for.

As with good names, it's hard to know exactly how bad these names are without some insider knowledge. All three suffered from some

---

[25] N. Statt. June 18, 2018. "Tronc to Change Name Back to Tribune Publishing After Years of Ridicule." *The Verge*. https://www.theverge.com/2018/6/18/17476412/tronc-tribune-publishing-name-change-la-times-sale
[26] N. Friedman. June 03, 2016. "Name in the News: Tronc." *Fritinancy*. https://nancyfriedman.typepad.com/away_with_words/2016/06/name-in-the-news-tronc.html

combination of dubious business decisions and poor communication; in each case, the name may have merely compounded an inevitable tragedy. But just as good brand names make good first impressions, bad names can set the wrong tone from day one. The fact that *Consignia*, *Qwikster*, and *Tronc* were so easily ridiculed—because they sounded bad, attempted to cram in too many ideas, fell victim to naming trends, or lacked relevant meaning—surely made matters worse.

CHAPTER 2

Types of Brand Names

Key Ideas

- Brand names are best classified along two dimensions: *naming approach* and *naming construct*.
- Approach ranges from *descriptive* to *suggestive* to *abstract;* construct includes *real-word, compound,* and *coined* names.
- The meaning, structure, and sound of a name contribute to its *tonality*, the feeling it evokes.

Around 2006, I was taking a lot of flights between Northern and Southern California. Almost without fail, I'd fly one of two airlines: Southwest Airlines or JetBlue, both U.S.-based low-cost carriers.

Given the price point,[1] it was tough for these brands to differentiate from one another, especially in such a highly regulated, low-margin industry. And yet, the two flying experiences always *felt* different to me. It wasn't just that JetBlue had TVs on the back of every seat and Southwest didn't. The brands had different personalities, which they effectively telegraphed through their respective brand names.

Southwest Airlines is a *descriptive* name; while they now carry more domestic passengers than any other U.S. airline, Southwest originally flew in Texas and adjacent southwest states. It's also a *real-word* name, given both *Southwest* and *Airlines* are real English words. And because the southwestern United States is known for sunshine and a laid-back culture, the descriptive name successfully evokes the brand's casual, warm personality.

---

[1] Back then, I could book a ticket for less than $40 each way—good news for a grad student in a long-distance relationship!

Because JetBlue began flying in 2000, specifically emulating Southwest's business model, they sought to distinguish themselves. In addition to the TVs and some blue potato chips, the JetBlue name is significantly different from Southwest's—it's a *compound*, created by fusing two real words. Although *Jet* is descriptive, *Blue* makes this a *suggestive* name by hinting at sky, friendship, loyalty, and, in the words of founder David Neeleman, "the wild blue yonder."[2]

Descriptive, real-word, suggestive, compound—these are four, simple ways of describing brand names. A quick Internet search reveals dozens of other so-called types of brand names, ranging from commonly used and easily understood terms such as *acronym, invented*, and *founder's name* to a number of less common, more obscure terms: *Amalgam. Deconstructed. Mimetic.*[3]

In fact, an almost infinite number of labels can be used to describe any brand name—they can be derived from *mythology*, contain *puns*, or employ *onomatopoeia*. But a long list of fancy words (see Figure 2.1) won't provide any clarity. Rather than simply labeling names, professional namers use a simple diagram to *classify* them—showcasing how various descriptors relate to one another. This system avoids the confusion created by self-proclaimed naming authorities who imply, for example, that *descriptive* and *real-word* are two separate types of brand names when, as discussed above, Southwest Airlines is an example of both. By understanding whether two terms are interchangeable, or one a subset of the other, we can form a clear, logical, and useful mental taxonomy of name types.

Classify Names by Approach and Construct

Rather than using a long, one-dimensional list of terms to describe different name types, organize names along two dimensions: naming *approach* and naming *construct*.

---

[2] R. Johnson. June 08, 2009. "JetBlue Airlines: It's All in a Name," *Travel + Leisure*. https://www.travelandleisure.com/travel-tips/jetblue-airlines-its-all-in-a-name
[3] See the glossary for definitions of these and other terms.

ABBREVIATION	DOUBLE-BARREL	LEXICAL
ABSTRACT	EMPTY VESSEL	MAGIC SPELL
ACRONYM	EVOCATIVE	MERGED
ALPHANUMERIC	EXPERIENTIAL	METAPHORICAL
AMALGAM	FABRICATED	MISSPELLED
APPROPRIATED	FANCIFUL	MIXED
ARBITRARY	FOUNDER'S NAME	MYTHICAL
ASSOCIATIVE	FUNCTIONAL	NEOLOGISM
BLENDED	GENERIC	ONOMATOPOEIA
COINED	GEOGRAPHICAL	PORTMANTEAU
COMPOSITE	GREEK ROOTS	REAL-WORD
COMPOUND	HISTORICAL	SIMPLEX
CONSTRUCTED	INITIALISM	SUGGESTIVE
DECONSTRUCTED	INVENTED	SYNECDOCHE
DESCRIPTIVE	LATIN ROOTS	TRUNCATED

Figure 2.1 Some of the many words used to describe brand names (see definitions of many of these terms in the glossary)

Approach, shown on the vertical axis in Figure 2.2, is a continuum from descriptive (bottom) to abstract (top), with a midrange commonly referred to as *suggestive*. The second dimension, construct, organizes brand names by how they're structured: real-word, compound, or coined. Professional namers can pinpoint almost any brand name by identifying its approach and construct. *Virgin* is an abstract, real-word name. *Febreze* is a suggestive, coined name. *Vitaminwater* is a descriptive, compound name. Next, we'll examine each dimension in more detail.

Naming Approach

The naming approach is about the *semantic* relationship between a name and an underlying brand—how the meaning of a name connects to the underlying company, product, or service. Approach can range from

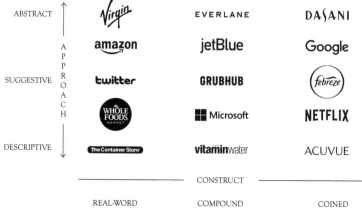

Figure 2.2 *Well-known brand names organized by naming approach and naming construct*

descriptive names, which tell it like it is, to abstract names, which have no relevant meaning. Many brand names are suggestive, falling somewhere between descriptive and abstract—they imply or hint at something about the underlying brand without coming right out and saying it. Often, the degree to which a suggestive name leans toward the descriptive or abstract end of the spectrum is debatable. Let's take a closer look at descriptive, abstract, and suggestive names, along with some examples.

Descriptive Names

Descriptive names clearly convey tangible information about the brands to which they refer. The Container Store is, indeed, a store that sells containers. Vitaminwater really does contain vitamins—although *Sugarwater* would be even more descriptive. The primary benefit of descriptive names is obvious: They require little or no explanation. Theoretically, less explanation means fewer resources expended clarifying what the company does or what the product is.

On the other hand, descriptive names (see examples in Figure 2.3) are less flexible and can pigeonhole a company that's outgrown its initial business model. Just look at Pizza Hut, which tried and failed to rebrand as *The Hut* in an effort to highlight non-pizza offerings (such as wings and pasta). RadioShack's attempts to become *The Shack* were no less doomed.

Figure 2.3 Well-known companies and products with descriptive names

Descriptive names are also typically less distinctive and harder to protect. Apple can stop another consumer electronics manufacturer from naming their company *Apple*, but they can't stop that company from using the word *watch* in the name of their Apple Watch knockoff.[4]

For these reasons, many professional namers advise against a descriptive approach at the company-name level. Moreover, a lot of people simply consider these names dull.[5] For example, a recent article in *Inc.* titled

---

[4] Then again, the fact that Apple can't stop anyone from using *watch* in their product name highlights another potential advantage of descriptive names—when viewed from the viewpoint of the Apple Watch knockoff manufacturer.

[5] I've heard two, half-joking analogies used again and again in efforts to discredit the descriptive naming approach. But on further reflection, neither stands up to scrutiny: (a) "If they'd used descriptive naming for sushi, we'd all be calling it 'cold, dead fish.'" In fact, *sushi* roughly translates to *pickled rice*. Originally, it was a descriptive name. (Not to mention the fact that most things we eat are dead, so I'm not sure why anyone would call that out in the name.) (b) "If descriptive names worked, Johnson & Johnson would call Band-Aids *bloody wound coverings*." Well, they would—and do!—call them *adhesive bandages*. The Band-Aid brand now includes products ranging from antiseptic wash to blister cushions.

"5 Pitfalls to Avoid in Naming Your Business" asserts, "While it may seem logical to give your business a name that describes exactly what it is, in doing so you're likely to wind up with something generic and, honestly, forgettable."[6]

But descriptive names can work well for products, services, and features, keeping the spotlight trained on more valuable brands (as evidenced by *Apple Watch*, which puts all the emphasis on the big brand—Apple). And even when naming a company, don't be so quick to write off the descriptive approach. Some descriptive names stand out via double entendre—such as *The Boring Company*, which bores holes—or surprising language—such as *Big Ass Fans*, which makes, well … big-ass ceiling fans.

Two special subcategories of descriptive names often *are* used as company names. In fact, go back far enough and seemingly all companies took one of two, literal approaches to naming: They adopted the name of their founder or the name of their place of origin.

Some of the oldest brands still around today have founders' names, such as Twinings Tea—founded by Thomas Twining in 1706.[7] Many world-famous brands follow this pattern, including McDonald's, Disney, and Louis Vuitton, and the use of founders' names is still pervasive today in banking, law, and other more traditional, stodgy industries.[8]

Other companies use geographic names, highlighting the country, city, or region in which they got their start. Founded near the Hudson Bay in Canada, Hudson's Bay Company now owns Saks Fifth Avenue, which is named for both its founder *and* the location of its flagship store. Other well-known brands with geographic names include Bank

---

[6] D. Kerpen. January 17, 2017. "5 Pitfalls to Avoid in Naming Your Business." *Inc.*, https://www.inc.com/dave-kerpen/5-pitfalls-to-avoid-in-naming-your-business.html

[7] Twinings claims to have the world's oldest unaltered logo in continuous use.

[8] Meanwhile, local businesses such as auto shops and bars are prone to using the *first* names of their founders or owners, as illustrated by Bob's Garage on *Schitt's Creek* and Moe's on *The Simpsons*.

of Taiwan, Nantucket Nectars, and New York Life. Many small, local businesses continue to use this descriptive approach today.[9]

Abstract Names

Truly abstract names don't even hint at what the brand is or does. Without additional context, no one could've guessed Starbucks sold coffee or Uber sold car rides. Abstract names may manage to convey some intangible quality, like a brand's personality, but they are untethered from any practical description of the underlying company or product.

Abstract names (see examples in Figure 2.4) are often easier to protect from a legal standpoint. They're also infinitely flexible, as evidenced by the fact a company that goes by *Virgin* can use that name for not only music, but across everything from banking to commercial spaceflight. On the downside, however, abstract names require more explanation due to their lack of inherent meaning, and therefore may take more time, effort, and money to build a brand around.

Bear in mind that *abstract* describes a naming approach but is agnostic with respect to construct. In other words, abstract names can be real words, like *Virgin*, or made-up words, like *Viagra*. Real-word abstract names are also known as *arbitrary*—what the United States Patent and Trademark Office (USTPO) describes as "actual words with a known meaning that have no association/relationship with the goods

---

[9] Note that not all people and place names are descriptive. The name *Tesla*, for example, is a nod to the prolific inventor and engineer Nikola Tesla, who died 60 years before the car company was founded. An homage like this is sometimes referred to as a *historical name*, but it is not descriptive. Nor is *Bombay Sapphire*, the name of a gin launched in England, by an English company. The name alludes to gin's popularity in India during the British Raj (which ended in 1947, about 40 years before the brand was born) and a famous sapphire known as the Star of Bombay (which, bafflingly, originated in Sri Lanka). In other words, the product has very little to do with Bombay. Given the branding world's obsession with authenticity, not to mention the fact that cultural appropriation is generally frowned upon, I've always been a little surprised this brand isn't more fiercely debated within the branding community.

Figure 2.4 Well-known companies and products with abstract names

protected."[10] Invented, abstract names are often called *fanciful* or *empty vessel* names—invented words with no definition, allowing the brand owner to pour meaning into them.

Suggestive Names

Sometimes referred to as *evocative* or *associative*, suggestive names (see examples in Figure 2.5) give clues as to what the brand is all about. Some give more obvious clues, such as *iPhone*, which doesn't really mean anything but clearly has something to do with phones. (The *i*, which originated in *iMac* and similar product names preceding the iPhone by almost a decade, was originally meant to convey *Internet*.) Suggestive names that fall toward the descriptive end of the spectrum are sometimes called *enhanced descriptive*.

On the other end of that spectrum, but still in the suggestive range, are names such as *Twitter*, which, according to cofounder and CEO Jack

---

[10] United States Patent and Trademark Office. n.d. *Protecting Your Trademark.* https://www.uspto.gov/sites/default/files/documents/BasicFacts.pdf

Figure 2.5 Well-known companies and products with suggestive names

Dorsey, means "a short burst of inconsequential information."[11] Despite Dorsey's admission that "that's exactly what the product was," it's hardly a descriptive name—without a lengthy explanation, no one could have guessed what a company or product named *Twitter* did. (The project's working name, *Status*, would have been far more descriptive, as the software allows users to share their personal status updates.)

Some brand names are described as *metaphorical*. By definition, metaphors are suggestive—they *suggest* a similarity or relationship in a nonliteral way. Therefore, metaphorical names are a subcategory of suggestive names. Most metaphors rely on real words—*Amazon*, for example, is a good metaphor for something massive, which was Jeff Bezos's vision for his online retailer. But compound and coined names can also contain metaphors.

Perhaps because it captures such a wide range of names, the suggestive category is "the most popular kind of brand name," according to

---

[11] D. Sarno. February 18, 2009. "Twitter creator Jack Dorsey illuminates the site's founding document. Part I." *Los Angeles Times*. https://latimesblogs.latimes.com/technology/2009/02/twitter-creator.html

Catchword, a leading naming agency in Oakland, California.[12] Suggestive names are also popular because they represent a compromise—they capture some benefits and avoid some drawbacks of the two extremes: descriptive and abstract.

Naming Construct

Naming construct is about structure, including whether a name is built from one or more real words, invented words, or parts of words mashed up to form something new. While naming approach is best conceptualized as a smooth continuum from descriptive to abstract, construct is typically conceived of as three discrete groups: real-word, compound, and coined names. Beyond these three groups, however, construct can also capture factors such as language (e.g., names with Latin roots), abbreviation (e.g., acronyms), use of numbers or symbols in names, capitalization, and length.

Real-Word Names

Real-word names are made up of one or more real, correctly spelled words. The U.S. food bank nonprofit Feeding America has a real-word name that more or less says what it is (i.e., a descriptive or enhanced descriptive name), while Quartz, the news organization, has a real-word, abstract name—because a crystalline mineral has nothing to do with business news.

Real-word names (see examples in Figure 2.6) are more likely to be spelled and pronounced correctly and have built-in meaning (for speakers of that language, at least). Real words also have connotations and associations that can cut both ways—positive connotations can redound to the brand's benefit while negative ones can torpedo an otherwise strong name candidate. Real-word names are also harder to acquire—if not from

---

[12] Catchword. n.d. *Creating the Perfect Name.* 3rd ed. https://catchwordbranding.com/wp-content/uploads/2016/03/CW_NamingGuide_100914.pdf

Figure 2.6 *Well-known companies and products with real-word names*

a legal standpoint, at least from the standpoint of digital real estate like web domains and social media handles.[13]

Some real-word names are actually phrases, such as *One Kings Lane* and *Fruit of the Loom*, or even full sentences, such as *I Can't Believe It's Not Butter!* and *Food Should Taste Good*. And a popular trend in naming involves combining real words or people's names (a kind of real word) with an *and*, sometimes signified by an ampersand or plus: Room & Board is a furniture store; Flour + Water is an Italian restaurant in San Francisco; Dolce & Gabbana is named after its founders, Domenico Dolce and Stefano Gabbana.

Compound Names

Compound names, also known as *composite, double-barreled, merged,* or *fused,* are created by connecting two or more real words—in their entirety—to form a new word. For example, *Zipcar* and *Fitbit* are each composed of two three-letter words. So is *PayPal,* but unlike the first two,

---

[13] The virtual impossibility of acquiring a simple, real-word web domain, however, shouldn't necessarily preclude you from using a real-word name. See Chapter 11 for more details on domain names.

it employs a *medial capital* on the second *P*—if you were to run your finger along the top of the name, you'd hit a hump in the middle—a pattern referred to as *internal capitalization* or *camel case.*

Compound names (see examples in Figure 2.7) are appealing because they allow namers to squeeze multiple ideas into a single name somewhat easily. *Zip* suggests something fast and easy, while *car* describes the product. *Fit* speaks to exercise and health; *bit* hints at something small, simple, and digital. Compared to real words, compound names can also be easier to lay claim to in terms of trademarks and web domains.

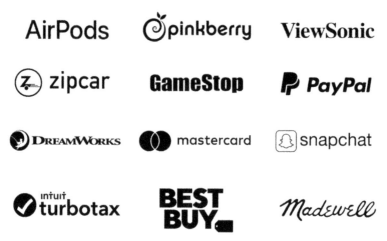

Figure 2.7 Well-known companies and products with compound names

Because of their ubiquity, compounds are sometimes said to *feel* like brand names. While this familiar feeling may provide some comfort when launching a new brand into the world, it can also result in a name feeling trendy or dated. Camel case, in particular, is associated with the late 90s and early 2000s, when companies like AltaVista and GeoCities reigned supreme. In the words of Amanda C. Peterson, former Head of Naming at Google, "There's no reason to use [camel case]. I think it's a crime against linguistics, personally."

Coined Names

Coined names include any that are made up of or contain newly invented words.[14] Sometimes referred to as *invented names, fabricated names,* or *neologisms,* this category includes all of the following constructs, arranged loosely from lightly coined to whole-cloth coinages:

- Misspelling or cacography: Flickr, Froot Loops, Lyft
- Portmanteau or blended name: Accenture (from *accent* and *future*), Groupon (from *group* and *coupon*), Pinterest (from *pin* and *interest*)
- Prefix/suffix: Instacart, Leafly, Spotify
- Truncation or deconstruction: Cisco (from *San Francisco*), Leidos (from *kaleidoscope*)
- Greek or Latin roots: Agilent, Diageo, Pentium
- Empty vessel or fanciful name: Exxon, Kodak, Dasani

Figure 2.8 Well-known companies and products with coined brand names

---

[14] Note, however, the subtle distinction between some coined names and compounds. Netflix, for example, would qualify as a compound name but for the deliberate misspelling of *flicks,* which makes it a coined name.

Generally, coined names (see additional examples in Figure 2.8) have the advantage of being more available, meaning they may be easier to trademark and protect and that domains and social media handles may be easier to obtain. But they're likely to be harder to spell, pronounce, and remember.

Coined names can work well for entirely new concepts, for which no suitable, real words exist. But a name without any built-in meaning—an empty vessel like *Exxon, Kodak,* or *Dasani*—may require more resources to educate target audiences and familiarize them with the name.

Let's take another look at our diagram, with some more name types and synonymous terms plotted.

As you can see in Figure 2.9, the two-dimensional, approach-construct classification system allows a deeper understanding of how different types of brand names relate to one another. *Coined* and *abstract* are not two, distinct name types, as the oversimplified, one-dimensional, *there are X types of brand names* formulation might lead you to believe. Rather, a single name can classify as both coined and abstract (like Kodak), a combination referred to as *fanciful* or *empty vessel*.

That said, while this system captures the vast majority of brand names, it fails to perfectly catch every brand name and name type.

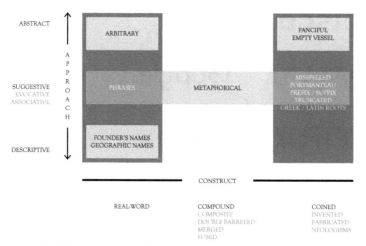

Figure 2.9 Many terms used to describe brand names can be mapped on the approach-construct diagram. Others are synonymous with the diagram's labels

Outliers

Some names are harder to classify; they don't fall squarely into any of our three, primary naming constructs or the naming approach they employ is up for debate. Rather than force-fitting them into our approach-and-construct diagram, it's often best to simply view these name types as outliers.

Abbreviations

If you're looking to show off your naming knowledge (and annoy your friends and colleagues), explain the difference between acronyms and initialisms: While often used interchangeably, acronyms are read and pronounced as words (e.g., *NASA*, the National Aeronautics and Space Administration), while initialisms are pronounced letter by letter (e.g., *IBM*, short for *International Business Machines*). Furthermore, some acronyms, referred to as *amalgams*, are formed from the first few letters of each word of a longer name, such as *Nabisco*, which is short for N*ational* Bis*cuit* Co*mpany*. Initialisms, on the other hand, use only the first letters—or *initial* letters—of each word in the longer name.

Rounding out the abbreviated name types are alphanumerics, distinguished by the combination of letters and numerals, and numerics—names and identifiers consisting of numerals only. Alphanumerics and numerics are often used to distinguish between products in large, complex portfolios, as Lexus does with cars like the UX 200 and LC 500h, or Boeing, with its 747 and 737 airplanes. But standalone products can also have alphanumeric names, like WD-40. So can entire companies, like 37signals, the original name of the organization behind the web-based project management tool, Basecamp.[15]

To understand why abbreviated names are sometimes hard to classify, let's look at a well-known company with an alphanumeric name: 3M. *3M* is not a real word. Arguably, it's not a coined word, either, because it's not

---

[15] *WD-40* is short for *Water Displacement, 40th formula*. 37signals is named after 37 radio telescope signals that may have been messages from aliens. And *Basecamp* is a great example of a suggestive, real-word name.

a word at all! That makes the naming construct hard to pin down, unless we create a new category for abbreviations.

The naming approach is not much easier. *3M* could be considered descriptive, because it's short for *Minnesota Mining and Manufacturing Company*. But many consumers of 3M products (like Scotch Tape and Post-it Notes) have no idea what those three Ms stand for—so it's likely *perceived* as an abstract name. The same is true of many abbreviated names. Just think: if you'd never known what *NASA* or *IBM* stood for, they'd be just as meaningless to you as *Altria* and *Exxon*.

That lack of inherent meaning is why, generally speaking, these abbreviated constructs (see Figure 2.10 for additional examples) are frowned upon by professional namers, especially for company names. Failing to convey any meaning on their own, they're like codes that customers must decipher. Furthermore, they're often bland, lacking in personality, and challenging from a spelling or pronunciation standpoint.

Figure 2.10 Well-known companies and products with acronyms, initialisms, amalgams, alphanumerics, and numerics for names

Foreign Languages

In naming, *real word* only applies to words from the primary language of the brand and its audience. *Tsingtao*, the name of a Chinese beer sold all over the world, might be considered foreign in the UK, but in China, it's simply a beer named after its place of origin: Qīngdǎo (青岛).[16] While words from one language are every bit as real as those from another, the distinction is important in naming because of how foreign words are perceived. And as with abbreviations, that perception depends heavily on the knowledge of the audience.

Some foreign language names are suggestive, using a language to convey attributes of the country in which it's spoken. Prego is a U.S.-born brand of tomato sauce, but it *sounds* Italian to Americans.[17] In other names, foreign words serve as empty vessels—chosen for how they sound or what they mean, even if there's very little chance their customers will pick up on that meaning. *Hulu*, for example, was chosen partly because "it is not a real word in the English language, and thus had no dictionary definition or immediate meaning in [the brand's] primary market," according to the company's former CEO.[18] (Also according to the CEO, *Hulu* means both *gourd* and *interactive recording* in Chinese.)

Prego and *Hulu* are real words in Italian and Chinese, respectively, but lumping them in with real-word names like *The Meatball Shop* and *Peacock* would fail to capture this unique name type. Adding yet another wrinkle, some brands use foreign-*sounding* names without using real foreign words. *Boku*, the name of a mobile payments platform, is an intentional misspelling of *beaucoup*, French for *very much*.

And then there's *Häagen-Dazs*. To many in the United States and around the world, it looks and sounds like a vaguely Danish name. But

---

[16] It's spelled differently because the romanization of Chinese characters has changed since the beer name was transcribed from Chinese to English.

[17] *Prego* is an Italian interjection that roughly translates to *You're welcome* or *Don't mention it*.

[18] *Lulu Enterprises Inc. v. N-F Newsite, LLC et al.*, U.S. District Court for the Eastern District of North Carolina Western Division, https://docs.justia.com/cases/federal/district-courts/north-carolina/ncedce/5:2007cv00347/90297/79

Danish writing does not use umlauts or the *zs* letter combination. The name is nonsense, invented in Manhattan by the Polish American founder, Reuben Mattus, who sat at his kitchen table and tried out different combinations of meaningless words until he heard something he liked.[19]

Tonality

In addition to differing based on approach and construct, brand names can vary in their *tonality*. Tonality is the feeling a name evokes. For example, LawGeex and DocuCollab, two contract management software companies, both have enhanced descriptive, coined names. But *LawGeex* is far more playful—silly, almost—while *DocuCollab* seems to take itself more seriously.

Tonality is related to a brand's *personality*, a set of human personality traits ascribed to a brand.[20] Often, a personality is formally articulated as part of a company or product's brand strategy. T-Mobile is fun, daring, genuine, and cool. Mozilla is gutsy, independent, open-minded, and "for good." Lyft is more cheerful than Uber.

When the brand personality hasn't been officially documented, it can usually be determined through a handful of interviews or a series of simple exercises. Regardless, namers need a general sense of the current or desired brand personality to ensure that it's reflected in the tonality of recommended name ideas. (Or, at the very least, that the tonality of the brand name does not clearly contradict the brand's personality.)

But what is it about the examples above—*LawGeex* and *DocuCollab*—that makes them feel silly and serious, respectively? Tonality is delivered through a combination of meaning, structure, and sound:

- **Meaning:** When brand names contain real words or recognizable parts of words, the definitions and connotations of those words can influence tonality. A name that contains *hyper*, for example, might be interpreted as energetic, powerful,

---

[19] *Boku* and *Häagen-Dazs* can easily be classified as coined names, but the fact that they're drawn from foreign or foreign-sounding words is notable.
[20] J.L. Aaker. 1997. "Dimensions of Brand Personality." *Journal of Marketing Research* 34, no. 3, pp. 347–356.

or intense—at least by speakers of English and any other languages in which *hyper* conveys a similar meaning (like Greek, from which English borrows the prefix).

- **Structure:** Short names might feel cute or clever, while longer names could feel heavy and important. Wordplay—like rhyming and alliteration—can make names feel more playful or whimsical (in addition to making them more memorable). Structure can impact tonality in many ways, but may more often act as a force multiplier on tonality conveyed through other attributes of a name.

- **Sound:** Sound symbolism, also known as phonosemantics, is the theory that speech sounds have meaning. Onomatopoeia is one example of sound symbolism—words like *whoosh* imitate a real-world sound. But individual letters and clusters of letters can also affect tonality. Many English words that begin with *sl* have something to do with water or moisture: slick, slime, slippery, slurp, slobber, slush, slurry, and slake, to name a few. As a result, names that begin with *sl*, whether real or coined words, may come across as sleek, smooth, or thirst-quenching.

Interestingly, because of sound symbolism, even an empty vessel name can have a tonality, despite its lack of inherent meaning. (You could argue, in fact, that empty vessel names trade on tonality alone.) In a classic psychology study,[21] participants were shown two shapes—one angular and one rounded—and asked to match them with names like *kiki* and *bouba*. You can try this experiment on yourself: Which of the shapes in Figure 2.11 would you guess goes with each name?

Figure 2.11 Examples of the kinds of stimuli used in studying the bouba/kiki effect. Which is which?

---

[21] W. Köhler. 1929. *Gestalt Psychology* (New York: Liveright).

If you called the jagged-looking shape *kiki* and the curvy shape *bouba*, your answers match those of the vast majority of respondents in these studies. Hard consonants like *k* and *t*, along with bright vowels (such as the *a* in *bat* or *ee* in *beet),* are associated with harder edges and sharper corners. Softer consonants like *m* and *l* and rounded vowels like the *a* in *wall* lend themselves to smoother, curvier forms.

Just as George Eastman liked *Kodak* for its powerful *k* sounds, Phil Knight was drawn to the strong sound of the *k* in *Nike*[22] (he was not immediately a fan of the name, however, as I'll explain in Chapter 8). And perhaps the soft *o* and *l* of *Olay*—a meaningless, coined name—contributed to its success as a beauty cream offering women softer, smoother skin.

---

[22] The strong sound of *k* also played a role in the selection of at least one other famous brand name: *Spanx.*

CHAPTER 3

The Basic Naming Process

Key Ideas

- A proven, rigorous process helps avoid many pitfalls of naming.
- The basic naming process includes seven steps, from creating a naming brief to a full legal search and final name selection.
- For a typical naming assignment, professional namers create hundreds of name ideas.

I'll admit it: my favorite scene in one of my favorite movies involves Scrabble. In the 1992 film *Sneakers*, Robert Redford's character leads a team of security professionals hired by people and companies "to break into their places, to make sure no one can break into their places." A pivotal scene halfway through the movie sees Redford flipping a Scrabble board and rearranging letters until he discovers that the name of a mysterious company is an anagram of *too many secrets*.

If you've never created a brand name, you may imagine the process a bit like that scene in *Sneakers*—a fun, late-night get-together in a room full of pizza, beer, brilliant minds, and Scrabble tiles. Maybe you've even heard tales of great brand names chosen that way, randomly selected from a hat full of employee suggestions, or by leafing through the pages of a dictionary.

In reality, while dumping the Scrabble board *could* lead to a great brand name—*New Relic*, after all, is an anagram of the founder's name, Lew Cirne—it's more likely to result in frustration and disappointment. Getting a group of people—with different backgrounds and goals—to agree on a handful of letters that are strategically optimal, legally available, and won't inadvertently offend an entire nation requires more

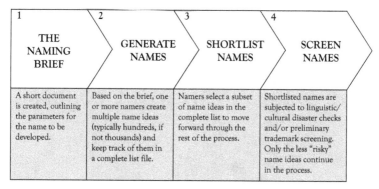

Figure 3.1 First four steps of the naming process

than creative brilliance and alcohol. It takes clarity, rigor, and—often—adherence to a proven process.[1]

Professional namers generally agree on the high-level naming process shown in Figures 3.1 and 3.2: create a brief, generate ideas (often hundreds), shortlist, prescreen, and present. If necessary, repeat. I've seen and used this process countless times in my 15-plus years as a namer, at agencies big and small, in the United States, Europe, and Asia, for naming everything from network security software to exotic vacation destinations. Different agencies and namers may take a few detours or throw their own spin on a step, but few venture too far from this best-practice approach.[2]

Parts II and III of the book will go into each step in more detail. For now, here's an overview of the seven-step naming process:

Step 1. The Naming Brief

The naming brief is usually a short document outlining parameters for the name. It is often a formal document but could be as little as scribbled notes from a one-hour brainstorm session. The brief should help the team

---

[1] Feel free to include some alcohol, too, however, assuming you're of age.

[2] Of course, as with any framework, the best and most experienced practitioners know how to modify it, customize it, or even scrap it entirely when appropriate for a given client or project.

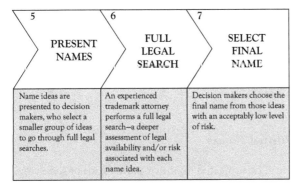

5 PRESENT NAMES	6 FULL LEGAL SEARCH	7 SELECT FINAL NAME
Name ideas are presented to decision makers, who select a smaller group of ideas to go through full legal searches.	An experienced trademark attorney performs a full legal search—a deeper assessment of legal availability and/or risk associated with each name idea.	Decision makers choose the final name from those ideas with an acceptably low level of risk.

Figure 3.2 Final three steps of the naming process

align on details like what the name should express, what approaches are acceptable (e.g., descriptive names), or what constructs are out of bounds (e.g., no coined words).

For more on the naming brief, see Chapter 4. For a naming brief template, turn to Part IV.

Step 2. Generate Names

Based on the approved brief, one or more namers create multiple name ideas—typically hundreds, if not thousands—and keep track of them in a single file that contains the complete list. Name generation can be conducted by individual namers, in a group setting, or some combination of the two. Ideally, multiple namers conduct multiple rounds of name generation to maximize the depth of exploration and diversity of ideas.

Chapters 6 and 7 go into detail on name generation.

Step 3. Shortlist Names

Namers select a subset of name ideas in the complete list to move forward through the rest of the process. When shortlisting and reviewing name candidates, the brief should serve as a guide to ensure a more objective consideration of ideas. Shortlisting is best played as a team sport—two or more namers should discuss the ideas, and it's sometimes useful to get some outside perspective from someone who didn't help generate names (ideally another experienced namer with an understanding of the assignment).

Shortlisting is pretty much as straightforward as it sounds, but for a few tips, turn to Chapter 8.

Step 4. Screen Shortlisted Names

Shortlisted names should be subjected to one or more forms of screening, depending on how the name will be used and where it will appear:

- Preliminary trademark screening involves searching trademark databases, like that of the U.S. Patent and Trademark Office (USPTO), for identical or similar marks used for similar goods or services.
- Linguistic and cultural disaster checks aim to uncover any potential pronunciation issues, negative connotations, or existing associations in languages and cultures around the world.
- Domain name availability can also be examined at this point, if applicable.

Ultimately, only those names deemed less risky will continue in the process.

Chapters 9, 10, and 11 cover trademark prescreening, linguistic checks, and domain name searches, respectively.

Step 5. Present Names

Decision makers review the names and select a smaller group of ideas—typically five or six—to go through full legal searches. Naming presentations often include some or all the following:

- A review of the naming brief
- An overview of the naming process to date, sometimes including the number of names generated and prescreened

- Some thoughts on how best to evaluate name ideas
- The recommended names, each with some rationale and mockups depicting the name in a realistic context (e.g., on a business card)
- A summary of names presented
- Next steps

Many naming projects include two or more rounds of naming, meaning steps two through five are repeated based on feedback on the presented names. For example, a team might select three names from the first naming presentation but decide to continue exploring the concept underlying one of them in the next round.

Chapter 12 is about the all-important naming presentation.

Step 6. Full Legal Search

Even when names have been through a preliminary trademark screening, an experienced trademark attorney should still perform a full legal search—a more in-depth assessment of legal availability and risk associated with each name idea. Full legal searches can take days or weeks, depending on the attorney's process and workload.

Chapter 13 goes into more detail on this step.

Step 7. Select the Final Name

At last, based on the brief, screening, legal assessment, and other factors, the decision makers choose the final name.

Selection is also covered in Chapter 13.

***

While following a solid process will help you avoid the foreseeable pitfalls of naming, it can't guarantee a great outcome—just as having the recipe for a gourmet meal doesn't make you a Michelin-starred chef. Experienced namers have an advantage at every step of this process, having learned through trial and error and honed their technique through repetition.

In Parts II and III, we'll dive deeper into each step, and I'll share tips and tricks I've picked up—either in my own naming career or by talking to other professional namers.

Review: Part I

Part I provided basic information on brand naming, such as why naming is important, what makes a good or bad brand name, how to classify the many types of brand names, and an overview of the seven-step naming process.

Chapter 1 highlighted the value of finding the right brand name, citing three reasons:

1. Language is powerful—a fact illustrated frequently in our personal lives and confirmed by scientific research.
2. Naming is hard, as evidenced by the perennial mocking of new brands by the press and public. Getting it wrong can be costly.
3. A good name is a good investment. It outlasts other marketing decisions, from ad campaigns to website redesigns, and it's a relatively inexpensive way to stand out in a crowded field of competitors.

While the effectiveness of a name depends on context and strategy, most good brand names strike a balance between strategic, creative, and technical qualities. Bad brand names usually lack these qualities and can also suffer from complexity, obscure references, or trendiness.

Chapter 2 described the clearest framework for classifying brand names, which requires two dimensions: naming approach and naming construct. Naming approach is about the meaning of a name as it relates to the company, product, or service being named. It ranges from descriptive to abstract, with suggestive falling somewhere in between. Naming construct describes the structure of the words making up a brand name. Common constructs are real-word, compound, and coined names. Abbreviations and foreign language names are outliers—harder to classify in terms of approach and construct. Tonality—the feeling a name evokes—should relate to the personality of the underlying brand and is conveyed through the meaning, structure, and sound of a name.

Chapter 3 provided a high-level overview of the naming process, seven steps designed to help mitigate common pitfalls of naming:

1. Creating a naming brief
2. Generating hundreds of names
3. Shortlisting the top name candidates
4. Screening shortlisted names (including preliminary trademark screening and linguistic/cultural disaster checks)
5. Presenting names
6. Having an experienced trademark attorney conduct a full legal search
7. Selecting the final name

PART II

Hundreds of Ideas

The best way to have good ideas is to have lots of ideas and throw away the bad ones.

—Linus Pauling,
Nobel Prize-winning chemist
and peace activist

CHAPTER 4

The Naming Brief

Key Ideas

- The naming brief documents important information, such as what ideas the name should convey.
- A good brief inspires creativity by clearly presenting a puzzle for the namer to solve.
- The brief is a critical first step in the naming process and should be approved by all relevant parties prior to name generation.

The naming brief points us in the right direction before we begin generating ideas. If you've heard the navigational wisdom that a very small error in heading will take you increasingly off course the farther you go, you'll understand why it's critical to get the naming brief right the first time around. If you reach the end of your long, metaphorical journey—a presentation of names, say—only to discover the brief pointed you off-course by one or two degrees, you'll be miles from your desired destination.

A typical naming brief is a short document—five or six pages or presentation slides—that outlines objectives and parameters for the name you're developing. Brainstorming name ideas without first articulating what the ideal name looks like is a recipe for disaster—especially when more than one decision maker is involved. The brief forces everyone to align on what the name should convey, what kinds of names to consider, and what's in and out of bounds. Ideally, every decision maker reviews and approves the brief before a single name is generated (step 2).

When shortlisting (step 3) and reviewing name candidates, the brief should be used as a guide to ensure ideas are considered as objectively as possible. In other words, it allows a team to evaluate names with reactions such as, *This name does an especially good job of expressing an idea from the brief* or *This name doesn't match the tonality described in the brief, because …* rather than more subjective, less useful reactions, like, *I don't like this name.*

According to Clive Chafer, Principal at Namebrand, failure to share the brief with someone who has veto power over the name is "the single biggest thing that goes wrong [in the naming process]." Inevitably, he says, when names are presented to that person, "he looks at it and goes, No. The answer is *no* because you didn't ask him what the question was in the first place—or involve him in getting to the answer."

What to Include in the Naming Brief

Agencies and namers typically have their own, preferred formats for naming briefs. Agency-specific and project-specific differences aside, however, most briefs contain the same, basic information:

A Description of What's Being Named

This could—and probably should—be a simple, layperson's explanation of the organization, product, or service to be named or renamed. A few bullet points may be enough, but more complex companies or offerings may require images, diagrams, or several paragraphs with links to additional information. A good question to answer here is, How would you explain this to someone you'd never met?

Ideas to Convey Through the Name

Sometimes called *naming territories* or *objectives*, these are arguably the most important points in the brief. Should the name make people think the thing you're naming is fast? Premium? Are you trying to convey a more abstract concept such as *connectivity* or *expansiveness*? Virtually every brand name expresses some underlying idea or emotion related to the product or organization it represents, even if only in a tenuous way. These ideas—often three or four per brief—can be captured in a list of words or phrases or fleshed out with short, explanatory paragraphs.

Naming Criteria (Approach and Construct)

Are you only interested in real English words? Or hoping for a name that's more suggestive than descriptive? This section of the brief defines which approaches and constructs are in-bounds and which are definitely out-of-bounds. These criteria can be represented by reproducing the approach-and-construct diagram from Chapter 2 and simply circling the area of exploration, striking out-of-bounds areas, or some combination of the two. This section of the brief should also specify whether words will likely be added before the name (e.g., a parent brand, like Nestle) or after (e.g., a descriptor, like *Chocolate*), whether the name is likely to be abbreviated, and other factors related to the name's construct.

For some projects, exploration of every construct and approach may be warranted and worthwhile. If that's the case, this section could still be useful in giving namers a sense of which areas to explore more heavily.

Name Tonality[1]

What feelings should the name evoke? What vibe should namers strive for—or avoid? If a brand personality has been defined as part of a broader brand strategy, list those traits here. Regardless, a description of the desired tonality or a list of attributes to aim toward (and away from) should be documented.

A Description of the Audience for the Name

What do we know about the people who'll be seeing or using this name? Ultimately, the name needs to work for them, and they may have knowledge, interests, or tastes that differ significantly from those creating and deciding on the name. The more clearly we can define the audience, the more we can get inside their heads when creating name ideas and making a final selection.

---

[1] For a reminder of what *approach, construct, tonality,* and other terms mean, see Part I, Chapter 2 or the glossary in Part IV.

Competitor or Peer Names

What names might be seen near this name, literally or otherwise? To avoid confusion (and trademark challenges), it's important to know the names of companies or products our brand will compete against. Beyond direct competitors, this section should include names of partner companies or adjacent products, vendor names, and any other names that could cause confusion or other problems.

Optional Information

In addition to the critical information above, many naming briefs also include some of the following, optional content:

- A project overview (e.g., timeline, milestones)
- Previously explored and rejected names, including details as to why any names were rejected
- Other brand names (in or out of category) the decision makers like, and why
- Domain name requirements or objectives—is an exact brand match dot-com domain required? If so, what budget has been allocated for acquiring a domain? If not, what other top-level domains are acceptable, and what descriptors could be added in order to acquire a satisfactory domain?[2]
- Lists of concepts, words, or word parts to explore or avoid
- Other brand strategy documentation (e.g., brand guidelines, brand book, brand platform, or brand positioning statement)
- Company naming guidelines, if they exist (relatively rare)
- Preliminary trademark screening criteria (e.g., what goods and services will be associated with the name, which informs the preliminary trademark screening process)
- Linguistic/cultural disaster check criteria (e.g., which countries/languages to review)
- Additional materials or links to review for background information

---

[2] See Chapter 11 for more information on domains and domain name availability.

What Makes a Good Naming Brief?

Not Too Loose, Not Too Tight

In 1969, Mick Jagger wrote a letter to Andy Warhol, offering him some guidance on creating "the art-work for our new hits album." Rather than explaining what he wanted the cover art to look like, Jagger simply told Warhol, "I leave it in your capable hands to do whatever you want."

Advertising professionals often reference this letter as an example of a creative brief and debate its merits—it's even been referred to as "the greatest brief ever written."[3] On the one hand, it gave Andy Warhol absolute creative freedom—exactly what every artist wants, right? On the other hand, it provided absolutely no information about what the Rolling Stones were hoping for, what they liked or didn't like, or what they wanted Mr. Warhol to think about when he was dreaming up ideas for the album cover.

It may have worked for Warhol, but with all due respect to The Stones, it's a *terrible* brief. The entire point of any brief is to provide constraints—guardrails within which creativity can flourish. The naming brief is no different. It needn't be a formal document, but it should contain some background information and guidance—some way for those generating ideas to know whether they're on the right track.

At the same time, the brief shouldn't overly constrain name generation. Imagine if Mick Jagger had written, "I want you to make the album cover a brightly colored, close-cropped screen print of my face, just like you did with Marilyn Monroe." At that point, why bother hiring the artist? His talent would have been wasted (and, I assume, he would've refused the project).[4]

The naming brief must strike a balance. It should inspire and tap into a namer's creativity, not stifle it. By providing details like the audience, ideas to convey, feelings to evoke, or what (if anything) is out of bounds, the brief should present a puzzle for the namer to solve—not just a list of boxes for the name to check.

---

[3] A. Berger (presentation, Talk NYC's ENGAGE: The NYC Digital Storytelling Conference, New York, April 10, 2013).

[4] Ultimately, Warhol created the cover art for a different album, "Sticky Fingers." It featured a man's crotch in jeans, complete with a working zipper.

Reviewed and Approved by All Relevant Parties

A few years back, I was sitting outside on the campus of a major entertainment company, waiting to present name ideas for a new app they'd been developing. I'd traveled to Southern California with my boss, who'd gone inside ahead of me to give our client's manager a quick progress update. My phone buzzed with a text: "He doesn't agree with the brief."

After weeks of coming up with names tailored to a brief we'd been told was greenlit by that manager, it sounded like we'd been barking up the wrong tree. Turns out our client hadn't shared the brief after all, probably because he considered his boss too busy or too important to bother until later in the process.

My client learned a lesson the hard way that day, and I learned it once again: it's critical to ensure anyone with decision-making or veto power reviews and approves the brief before naming begins. Similarly, anyone involved in selecting or approving names should attend naming presentations, so they're immersed in the process and understand the context around each name idea. Don't send name ideas in an e-mail. Don't forward naming presentations to people who didn't attend the meeting. And don't let someone else present your name ideas unless you're confident they'll do them justice.

Includes Some Real Names or Name Ideas

Where possible, use real names and name ideas in the naming brief. Along with abstract ideas you're hoping the name will express, be sure to include a few tangible examples—other names in the marketplace that the decision makers like or dislike and any name ideas that have been considered or rejected previously. It's easy for a team to agree the name should sound *modern* or *pithy*—but once you're looking at realistic names, you may find everyone interprets those ideas a bit differently.

How to Create the Brief

As stated above, the naming brief can be a relatively formal or informal undertaking. The approach to creating the brief, therefore, varies from project to project. As part of a more structured naming process, it might include some or all of the steps below. In a less formal environment, the following steps may still be useful, although each may be more cursory than the text below suggests. (For example, conducting research might consist of a quick web search.)

Conduct Research

If a brand strategy has already been articulated—a brand platform, positioning statement, or vision and mission, say—it can often form the basis of the naming brief. If not, you'll need to conduct some research, which could include reviewing marketing materials, business strategy documents, or survey data. Often, a handful of one-on-one interviews (e.g., with company leaders or product managers) and a review of some relevant websites is enough to get started.

Ultimately, writing a useful and accurate brief will require you to confidently answer questions about what's being named, what's known about the audience for the name, and what names are in use by competitors or peers. Your research should include whatever it takes to find solid answers to those questions.

Write a First Draft

Put together a rough draft of the naming brief, including all pertinent information. If useful, start with a naming brief template like the one provided in Part IV of this book.[5] The brief should contain enough text to explain ideas clearly while remaining succinct and avoiding redundancies.

Share the Draft

Seek reactions to the brief from others. If you're working alone, you'll find it useful to get an outside perspective, ideally from someone with knowledge of what you're naming and a well-informed understanding of branding. Be wary of any absolutist advice on names, however—there

---

[5] You can also download a free naming brief template at brandnamingbook.com/downloads.

are plenty of pet theories out there about letters every successful brand name must contain, or types of names that invariably work better than others. At least for now, it's best to ignore this conventional wisdom and dogma—anyway, it's often hyperbolic and sometimes dead wrong.

If you're working with a team of decision makers, you can share the brief via formal presentation, perhaps along with *reality check* names (see below), or simply send it via e-mail and invite the team to discuss by phone.

Share Some Reality Check Names

This step is not always needed but can provide deeper insights into whether the brief will help lead to a satisfactory name. Reality check names, sometimes called *trial balloons* or *checkpoint names*, are simply initial name ideas that have not been screened for legal or linguistic challenges, used to check that the brief is clear and unlikely to be misinterpreted. Sharing reality check names can be risky—to avoid letting a decision maker fall in love with a potentially unavailable name idea, your presentation should be littered with caveats. Remind everyone that anything shared at this stage is for illustrative purposes only. These name ideas may not be—and in many cases, probably aren't—available for use.

The purpose of reality check names is to probe some of the abstract language in the brief and get decision makers to react to something more tangible. For example, a team might agree that the brand name being developed should sound *fun*. Upon seeing a few reality check ideas, however, they may be able to further define what they mean, as some ideas you present may be deemed too strait-laced, ridiculous, or offensive to meet the team's definition of *fun*. By analyzing reactions to reality check names, you can fine-tune the brief.

For the same reason, you can also use this step to present some names that push the envelope with respect to the brief. Using the example above, finding the sweet spot between *not fun enough* and *too fun* may require examples that run the gamut, including some you'd be wary of presenting as real recommendations. If you plan to push the envelope, it's best to share this information up-front: *Some of the ideas I'm about to show you are designed to provoke a response.*

Revise and Finalize

Based on reactions and feedback, iteratively revise the brief until all decision makers approve its contents. In some organizations, that may mean moving out in concentric circles or up the food chain, sharing drafts of the brief with increasingly large teams or senior decision makers as you revise.

Secure Approval

Ensure all decision makers have reviewed and approved the brief prior to commencing name generation. Some situations call for written approval or sign-off, while others allow for a less formal go-ahead.

CHAPTER 5

Getting Set Up

Key Ideas

- Preparation for name generation includes setting up a complete list file and determining who will contribute name ideas.
- For most projects, the ideal naming team consists of a handful of experienced namers, each dedicating multiple hours to name generation, working separately but meeting repeatedly to compare notes and divvy up remaining work.
- Basic principles of ideation and brainstorming—including *Go for large quantities of ideas* and *No criticism of ideas*—work well as ground rules for name generation.

While it's tempting to dive straight in and start coming up with name ideas, you'll thank yourself later for first taking some simple steps to prepare.[1] Let's examine three ways to get ready for a successful naming project: setting up your complete list file, determining who will generate names, and reviewing some basic ideation ground rules.

The Complete List File

Throughout a naming project, keep a complete list of every idea generated. Whether you start out with a pad and pen, a whiteboard, or a series of e-mails or texts, make sure to collect every idea—not just your favorites—in one place. Many namers record name ideas in spreadsheet software (e.g., Microsoft Excel, Google Sheets, or Airtable), which makes

---

[1] That said, be sure to jot down any initial ideas, lest you forget them.

Table 5.1 Example rows from a complete list spreadsheet

Namer	Name ideas	With following text	Notes
MB	Bishop	Bishop Astronomy	
DC	Temper	Temper Astronomy	
GJ	Setec	Setec Astronomy	*Anagram*
MR	Apollo	Apollo Astronomy	

for easier sorting, de-duplication, and recording of notes associated with each name.[2]

To set up a complete list spreadsheet, create headers for simple sorting and filtering. As depicted in Table 5.1, label one column *Name ideas* and another *Notes*, where you'll have the option of adding details like the origin or rationale behind a name idea. If multiple people are generating names, track who suggested each idea in a *Namer* column. This isn't to give credit to whoever came up with the final name, but to make it easier to ask questions about name ideas, if needed, later in the process.

In projects where the name will likely be paired with another brand name or word—for example, preceded by a parent brand name (like *Hyundai* before *Ioniq*) or followed by a descriptor (like *Books* after *Penguin*)—create a column to test out these pairings without having to type them over and over again. In a spreadsheet, you can create and drag a formula to automatically combine relevant words.[3]

Tracking name ideas in spreadsheet software also allows you to easily find duplicates. When multiple namers are working to generate hundreds of ideas, you're bound to see a handful of ideas more than once. Find these duplicate entries by sorting the name ideas alphabetically or—better yet—setting up *conditional formatting*, which can automatically highlight any redundant name ideas as soon as they're entered. But don't delete duplicates without first noting that two or more namers came up with

---

[2] To download a free complete list spreadsheet template with sortable columns, example content, and built-in highlighting of duplicate entries, visit brandnamingbook.com/downloads.

[3] For example, =CONCATENATE("Hyundai ",B2) or =CONCATENATE (B2," Books").

the same idea, which can prove useful when shortlisting or discussing the relative merits of names.

The Naming Team

Building a team to generate names is all about striking the right balance. Leave it all to one person, and you'll get fewer ideas with no diversity of thought. But if you open it up to hundreds of employees, it starts to feel like crowdsourcing or a naming competition rather than a focused effort.

If many heads are better than one, what's wrong with crowdsourcing or running a public naming contest, you ask? Answers include Boaty McBoatface,[4] Mister Splashy Pants,[5] and The Harry Baals Government Center.[6] If these real-life results from public naming contests aren't enough to scare you off, consider the fact that naming contests typically suffer from minimal structure, a lack of direction at the outset, and namers without experience or expertise. Crowdsourcing ideas—whether in a contest format or not—can also lead to just one entrant feeling validated; everyone else involved may feel slighted when their brilliant idea isn't even acknowledged, much less chosen. That said, taking a more-the-merrier approach during name generation can pay off, as long as it's within the guardrails of a structured naming process.

Relatedly, think carefully about time allocation. One large agency I worked for seemed to believe the best way to staff a naming project was to ask for an hour each of name generation from a dozen namers. The opposite is closer to the truth. While more heads are better than one, an hour simply isn't enough time to dig deep on a naming project and get past the most obvious ideas. If you're divvying up 12 hours, 4 hours each

---

[4] K. Rogers. March 21, 2016. "Boaty McBoatface: What You Get When You Let the Internet Decide." *The New York Times.* https://www.nytimes.com/2016/03/22/world/europe/boaty-mcboatface-what-you-get-when-you-let-the-internet-decide.html

[5] K. Nicol. December 11, 2007. "Mr. Splashy Pants and the Tale of a Hijacked PR Campaign." *Mashable.* https://mashable.com/2007/12/12/mr-splashy-pants-greenpeace/

[6] "Scratch 'Harry Baals' off List of Names for Government Center." *NBC News.* February 08, 2011. https://www.nbcnews.com/id/wbna41480994

from 3 experienced namers will net better results than 1 hour each from 12 people.

Ultimately, much of name generation is a solitary pursuit, best conducted with easy access to reference works and online tools. With Wikipedia[7] and a thesaurus just a keyboard away, a focused namer can get into a flow,[8] transcend the expected, and begin to perform the lateral thinking required for true creativity. Group settings, by contrast, are less conducive to deep thinking and creative courage—they often result in lackluster ideas and leave everyone feeling like more exploration is needed.

Team brainstorm sessions have their place, however: When first examining a naming brief, for example, a team can work together to think through alternative territories to pursue. In a brief asking for names that express *light as a feather*, a team might collectively think of associations and metaphors—aircraft, celestial bodies, atmospheric phenomena, pastel colors, a perfect pastry, flying animals—and then assign each of these to a different namer for further exploration. It's also useful to meet as a group midway through name generation to compare notes and discuss challenges before continuing. For the best results, naming teams should repeatedly get together, decide on next steps, divide and conquer, then meet up again, and so on. Multiple namers conducting multiple rounds of name generation, working *together but separately*, will maximize the depth of exploration and diversity of ideas.

Ideation Ground Rules

While naming is unique in many ways, it still adheres to some basic rules of creative exercises. In 1939, James Webb Young published *A Technique for Producing Ideas*, a short handbook in which he proposes a five-step process for coming up with good ideas.

---

[7] The *wiki* in *Wikipedia* is a Hawaiian word meaning *quick*.
[8] A concept named and popularized by psychologist Mihály Csíkszentmihályi in his 1975 book, *Beyond Boredom and Anxiety: Experiencing Flow in Work and Play*.

James Webb Young's Five Steps for Producing Ideas[9]

1. Gather raw material: Collect and organize any relevant information you can get your hands on.
2. Digest the material: Read, observe, think about, and analyze what you've collected. Where possible, group things and make connections between groups. Try ideas on for size.
3. Unconscious processing: Step away from the information for a while and try to stop thinking about the problem.
4. Wait for the *a-ha moment*: Often, ideas will bubble up from the subconscious. Be ready to capture them (e.g., by writing them down or recording them).
5. Introduce the idea to reality: Try implementing the idea. See what works and what doesn't. Revise, refine, and fine-tune accordingly.

Young worked in advertising (an original *Mad Man*), but his rules apply equally well to naming. Steps 3 and 4, especially, ring true and foreshadow passages in later chapters of this book.

We can also thank the advertising world for the ubiquitous *rules of brainstorming*, which you may have encountered in past workshops or creative sessions. Created by Alex Osborn, the *O* in global advertising agency BBDO, these four rules serve as useful guideposts for any creative endeavor.

Alex Osborn's Four Rules of Brainstorming[10]

1. No criticism of ideas
2. Go for large quantities of ideas
3. Build on each other's ideas
4. Encourage wild and exaggerated ideas

---

[9] J.W. Young. 1940. *A Technique for Producing Ideas*. Chicago: Advertising Publications, Inc.

[10] A.F. Osborn. 1953. *Applied Imagination: Principles and Procedures of Creative Thinking* (New York: Scribner).

As mentioned above, group brainstorms have limited benefits when generating name ideas. But these rules can help you get the most out of individual work, too: Don't criticize your own ideas. Don't be too quick to filter out your weakest ideas before others have seen them, as they may spark new thinking. And build on your own ideas—go back through your list occasionally to see if you can modify a previous idea or combine two ideas.

Osborn's second rule, *Go for large quantities*, is especially relevant to naming: at first, quantity is the main goal. A professional namer will shoot for at least 100 ideas per round, and typical naming projects involve hundreds—if not thousands—of name ideas. As Amanda C. Peterson, former Head of Naming at Google, puts it, you're looking for "quality *through* quantity." More ideas can lead to better ideas, and the need for quantity will become even more clear when you begin subjecting names to trademark prescreening and linguistic searches.

CHAPTER 6

Basic Name Generation

Key Ideas

- Name generation begins with words in the brief and expands through explorations of synonyms, metaphors, related ideas, and subterritories.
- Namers can dive deeper through creative thinking exercises such as *conceptual spelunking*, in which they imagine themselves exploring caves full of concepts.
- Skilled namers conduct research—online and off—looking for lists, glossaries, and reference articles that can lead to interesting name ideas.

There is no *right way* to generate name ideas—no more than there is a right way to paint a canvas or cook a gourmet meal. But, as with painting and cooking, naming comes with some reliable best practices. In other words, despite its comparatively short history, professional naming has its equivalents of color theory and knife skills.

The aim of this and the following chapter is therefore not to prescribe a single, best way of coming up with names but to share common methods and generally accepted techniques. By shedding light on how professional namers tackle name generation today, the recommendations in these pages may strengthen your process, augment your name generation toolbox, or open your eyes to different ways of thinking about brand names. Once you've learned the basics, feel free to build on or modify them to suit your needs and your personal style. In the words of Benjamin Dreyer, managing editor of Random House and author of *Dreyer's English*, "As much as I like a good rule, I'm an enthusiastic subscriber to the notion of 'rules are meant to be broken'—once you've learned them, I hasten to add."[1]

Our Hypothetical Naming Assignment

To better demonstrate the recommended steps in this chapter and the next, I'll use a hypothetical naming brief seeking a name that conveys three ideas: *strong*, *fast*, and—to build on an idea mentioned in Chapter 5—*light as a feather*. These are common naming territories that could apply to a range of companies or product categories, from medical devices to running shoes. For the purpose of this example, let's say it's a laptop that's billed as a MacBook Air killer.

In practice, briefs may request names that speak to more abstract ideas than strength, speed, and weight—*connectivity* or *discovery*, for example—or more specific, tangible ideas like *financial security* or *coffee flavor*. I've chosen *strength*, *speed*, and *lightness* as a comfortable midpoint between abstract and tangible, but the steps below apply equally well anywhere along this spectrum.

Start With the Brief

Whether it's a formal document, an e-mail thread, or notes from a conversation, the naming brief should provide multiple jumping-off points for name generation. Read it once, then go through it again, noting any potential names, parts of names, or key concepts for the name to convey.

Capture your initial ideas, grouping them by naming territories. Starting with our hypothetical brief, for example, you could represent each territory—*strong*, *fast*, and *light as a feather*—as a mind map, a cluster of sticky notes on the wall, or a column in a spreadsheet.[2] Once you've exhausted ideas pulled straight from the brief and any other early ideas, start thinking about synonyms, etymologies, metaphors, and other concepts related to those in the brief. To expand your thinking, call on resources

---

[1] B. Dreyer. 2019. *Dreyer's English* (New York: Random House).

[2] Be sure to use a new tab if you're working in a complete list file.

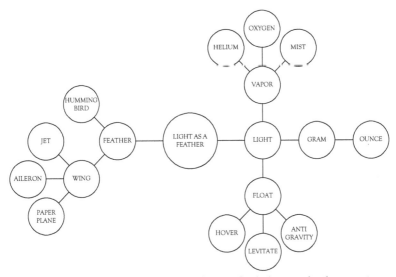

Figure 6.1 An initial mind map exploring the **light** **as a feather** *territory*

like a thesaurus or Google Search.[3] Continue adding ideas, keeping them organized around conceptual territories. Eventually, you may find you've opened up a new territory, landed on a useful subterritory, or discovered a new way of looking at a territory from the brief. If so, create a new grouping (e.g., a new mind map or spreadsheet column) to further explore that angle.

Let's try it out. While exploring *light as a feather*, you might create a mind map containing your initial ideas, as shown in Figure 6.1.

Looking at a handful of ideas in that first pass, including **Hummingbird** and **Jet**, you may realize you've veered into a new territory or subterritory for *light as a feather*—call it *things that fly*. To keep your thoughts organized and give yourself space to pursue this subterritory further, create a new mind map, group of sticky notes, or spreadsheet column, and continue adding relevant ideas there. See Figure 6.2.

While it's easiest to start by considering each territory in isolation, note that most of the ideas in this list have the added benefit of speaking to *fast* and *light as a feather* simultaneously. Combining the lists in Figures 6.1 and 6.2, we've already generated 30 name ideas. (And remember, we're focused on quantity at this point. While **Housefly** certainly

---

[3] See the list of naming resources in Part IV.

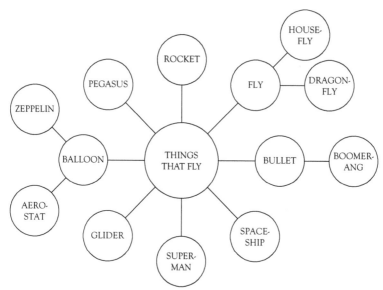

Figure 6.2 **A mind map exploring** things that fly, *a subterritory of* light as a feather

has some negative connotations, it's important to avoid second-guessing yourself until later in the process.) What's more, many of the ideas above could easily give rise to additional ideas or sub-territories:

- **Helium**: Other lighter-than-air gasses like **Hydrogen** and **Neon**
- **Gram**: Other small units of measurement like **Cubit** (an archaic unit of length) and **Arc** (as in *10 seconds of arc*)
- **Hummingbird**: Other species of birds or parts of birds (aside from **Feather** and **Wing**, which are already on the list) like **Osprey** and **Alula** (Latin for *winglet*, a small part of a bird's wing also known as a *bastard wing*)
- **Boomerang, Bullet**: Other projectiles like **Missile** and **Dart**
- **Superman**: Other flying heroes like **Hawkman** and **Starfire**[4]

---

[4] Note, however, that hewing too closely to the names of famous fictional characters could easily lead to trademark or copyright concerns. But at this point in the process, you should still be operating in *no criticism of ideas* mode.

Given we've only scratched the surface of one of three territories in the brief, it's easy to see how an experienced namer could quickly create a list of over a hundred name ideas.

Diving Deeper

Building a solid list of names often comes down to finding interesting, unexpected ways of conveying ideas (or tonalities, in the case of abstract names). To that end, any method of spurring creative, lateral, or divergent thinking can lead to interesting name candidates, including the following:

- Freewriting: This is the practice of writing down everything that pops into your head without worrying at all about whether you think it's good or even makes sense.
- Random entry: Introduced by Edward de Bono in his seminal book, *The Use of Lateral Thinking*, this technique involves picking a random idea from a dictionary, encyclopedia, or elsewhere and seeing whether you can somehow connect it back to your naming assignment. Upon randomly selecting the word *stone* from a book, we might come up with **Stoneskipper**, since skipping stones seem to be lighter than air, or a song by the Rolling Stones, like "Wild Horses"—**Wildhorse** could be an interesting way of suggesting speed.
- Provocation: Another Edward de Bono recommendation, a provocation is an impossible statement—something like *The spaceship flies underwater*—used to provoke unexpected ideas. A submarine is a bit like an underwater spaceship—thinking that could lead to ideas such as **Alfa**, a class of super-fast Russian subs.

Conceptual Spelunking

Since naming deals with words, however, it's useful to spend some time thinking about how words capture meaning and how meanings are related to one another. Anthony Shore of Operative Words describes this well in his blog post, "How to Name: Explore Concepts, not Words."[5] Anthony relates name generation to "an actual expedition." Imagine yourself standing in a cave that represents a concept from the brief. You can move *up* to a parent concept or category (called a *hypernym* in linguistics), *down* to child concepts or subordinates (*hyponyms*), and *across* to coordinate or sibling terms (*allonyms*).

For example, beginning with *red*, we can figure out what to move up to by completing the sentence, *Red* is a type of _____. *Color* is the most obvious parent concept, of course. But *wine* could also work, and it might land us somewhere interesting.[6] From *wine*, we can look for sibling terms by asking, "With what can we group *wine* in a category?" Well, we could easily pair our *wine* with *juice* in the *beverage* category. To move down from there, we can ask, "What are some types of *juice*?" And, remembering where we started—seeking ways to express *red*—we find *pomegranate*, *tomato*, and maybe *Bloody Mary*. Like that, we've landed on an interesting, spicy expression of *red*.

Let's try it with our brief. This time we'll look at *fast*, as shown in Figure 6.3. *Fast* is a type of *property*. We've moved up. From there, we can go across to *ability*, a related concept. What are some types of abilities? A quick Internet search brings up a list, which includes *communication* and *art*. Staying mindful of our initial concept, *fast*, we can drill down to some fast forms of communication: A **Gesture** or **Pictogram** can convey meaning instantaneously. From *art*, we might have to drill down two levels—first to *drawing* and *music*, then, still seeking ways to express *fast*, another level to **Sketch** and **Scribble**—both drawing techniques—and **Bebop**, a fast form of music. For me, **Bebop** evokes a blistering tempo, syncopated rhythms, and impossibly quick-witted improvisation. In other words, an interesting, unexpected way of capturing *fast*. (And come to think of it, **Tempo**'s not a bad idea either.)

This method can be repeated with any relevant concept or word from the complete list file. Let's try it with **Rocket**, asking ourselves questions that help us conceptually travel up, down, and across:

---

[5] A. Shore. October 03, 2018. "How to Name: Explore Concepts, not Words." *Operative Words Blog.* https://www.operativewords.com/blog/2018/6/12/3kxk51nliieab9jxsss3xwg9vas7w0

[6] A trick here: Try typing *Red is a type of* into Google Search, and see how it autocompletes your query.

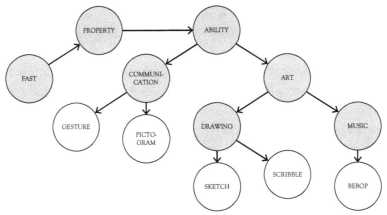

Figure 6.3 A visual depiction of conceptual spelunking

- Up
  - A rocket is a type of _____? ***Engine***, ***Projectile***
  - A rocket is a part or aspect of _____? An ***Arsenal***, a ***Spacecraft***
- Across
  - Rocket and _____ are both types of (engines or projectiles)? ***Hydraulic*** or ***Harpoon***
  - Besides a rocket, another part of a(n) (arsenal or spacecraft) is a _____? ***Ammunition*** or ***Orbiter*** (the technical name for the airplane-like component of the Space Shuttle)
- Down
  - A type of rocket is _____? ***Plasma***, ***Saturn*** (rockets used on Apollo missions)
  - A part or aspect of a rocket is _____? ***Propellant***, ***Fin***

Research

Diving deeper can also mean taking the time to conduct research on a relevant topic. As you can probably guess, executing the conceptual spelunking exercises above required me to do some quick desktop research on juice, abilities, communication, drawing, music, rockets, and bird wings. (No, the word *alula* isn't really part of my everyday vocabulary.)

Online searches such as *forms of communication* or *fast styles of music* will produce long lists and reference articles that are invaluable in helping complete the exercise and reap its rewards.

But research need not be limited to specific exercises—online and offline research can supplement name generation at any stage. For example, in exploring *strength* from our fictional brief, we might decide to look at *armor* as a metaphor, leading to an in-depth investigation of the history of armor, types of armor, and materials used in armor—research that could uncover ideas like **Ironclad**, **Bulletproof**, and **Titanium**, respectively. To find these deeper ideas, namers often seek out lists, glossaries, technical documents, and encyclopedia entries. It's also why some namers have shelves lined with esoteric textbooks and reference works.[7]

This kind of research can take namers down rabbit holes. Some lead to breakthroughs. Others are dead ends. It's part of why some professional namers insist on four hours of focused name generation, minimum, to crack an assignment. For most namers, leaving no stone unturned is a point of pride. To build a list that goes beyond the most obvious ideas and gets into more interesting, diverse, and unexpected territory, try diving deeper.

---

[7] See The Namer's Bookshelf in Part IV for a long list of books used by professional namers.

CHAPTER 7

Building Out the List

Key Ideas

- To build out the name list, namers employ techniques that draw on wordplay, outside inspiration, new angles of attack, purposeful distraction, or other methods of breaking through writer's block.
- Books and online tools like a dictionary, thesaurus, language dictionary, word combiner, or word solver can help augment a name list.
- Because the primary goal at this point is quantity, the complete list will inevitably contain a mix of good and not-so-good ideas.

Because the goal is quality *through* quantity, you'll sometimes want to take advantage of a few other, simple, low-hanging-fruit techniques for name generation. Some of these only work for naming briefs that allow for coined, compound, or non-English names—they won't be a good fit for every naming project. Others may feel a bit cheap and can give rise to the type of trendy, clichéd name that professional namers love to hate. But in keeping with our *no criticism of ideas* brainstorming rule, at least in the early stages of name generation, anything is fair game. And you never know; you may stumble upon something useful.

On the following pages, I've listed 18 techniques, each demonstrated using our fictional naming brief and some name candidates generated in Chapter 6. For the purposes of these examples, let's assume our naming brief allows for any naming construct—real-word, compound, or coined—and that tonality is out the window.

Wordplay

Mix and Match Words or Word Parts to Create Novel Compound Names

Try combining short words from your complete list to create compound name ideas. You can do this manually or use an online tool that takes words from two or more lists and combines them in every possible way.[1] By feeding lists of monosyllabic words like *light*, *fly*, and *dart* into one of these tools, we can discover a handful of interesting candidates:

- *Lightwing*
- *Superfly* (a real word—and a movie—but in this case, pulled from *Superman*[2] and *Fly*)
- *Dartbird*

Combine With Common Words and Word Parts

Fuse ideas from your list with common prefixes, suffixes, Greek or Latin roots, or short words. Look up lists of roots or morphemes (the smallest meaningful units of a language[3]) and try them on for size. Again, online tools can speed this process up. Watch out, however, for trendy suffixes like *ly* and *ify*, which can result in trite, forgettable, and quickly dated names.[4] Greek and Latin roots, when their usage feels forced, have also earned a bad reputation in naming due to a few high-profile concoctions from the late 90s and early 2000s, like *Diageo* and *Altria*.[5]

---

[1] Search online for a *keyword combiner*, and a variety of free tools will pop up.

[2] Here's an example of why *Superman* shouldn't be discarded immediately due to probable copyright and trademark issues. By leaving it on the list, we can use it to generate additional, less problematic ideas.

[3] A prefix like *tri*, which conveys meaning in a single syllable, is a morpheme. It cannot be divided into smaller meaningful units.

[4] In case you missed it, a footnote in Chapter 1 mentioned Nancy Friedman's Pinterest board of 300+ names ending in *ly*, including *Bitly*, *Insightly*, and *Optimizely*.

[5] *Diageo* combines a Latin word, *dies*, meaning *day*, with a Greek word, *geo*, meaning *world*. The intended meaning of the full name is echoed in the company's tagline, *Celebrating Life, Every Day, Everywhere*. *Altria* is based on the Latin word *altus*, meaning *high*, to suggest high performance (of the stock, perhaps). But some—including Harvard linguist Steven Pinker—have also noted the name's similarity to *altruism*.

- *Avimist* (*Avi* is a Latin root used in words relating to birds or flight.)
- *Flyology*
- *Floatable*

Lightly Coin by Altering Spelling or Adding, Removing, or Changing Letters

As mentioned in Chapter 2, the art of coining names can range from inventing words whole cloth, like Häagen-Dazs, to simply misspelling a word on purpose (cacography). Try a lighter approach to coining by slightly modifying name candidates in your list. Don't forget to try breaking words apart to form truncated or deconstructed names like *Cisco*.

- *Zoomerang*
- *Oxy* (shortened from *Oxygen*)
- *Fynn*

Explore Other Languages

Whatever your native language (or, perhaps more importantly, the native language of your name's audience), use your knowledge of other languages, language dictionaries, and translation software like Google Translate to find interesting, relevant words.

- *Avion* (French for *plane*—note that it makes use of the Latin root, *avi*)
- *Uku* (Japanese: *float*)
- *Umoya* (Zulu: *the wind*)

Look for Rhymes or Other Forms of Wordplay

Use a rhyming dictionary (online or off) and other tools to find opportunities to rhyme, alliterate, create portmanteaus, or employ other forms of wordplay. Online word finders and solvers (e.g., OneLook Dictionary Search) can help immensely here. To find some alliterative names based on *Float*, we can search for other words beginning with *fl* and find *flex*, creating **Floatflex**. And, seeking a portmanteau based on **Wing**, we can search for words beginning with rhymes like *thing* and find *thingamajig*, leading us to **Wingamajig**.

- *Floatflex*
- *Wingamajig*
- *Bellfeather* (from *bellweather*)

Outside Inspiration

If the techniques above seek to build on your existing work—combining, modifying, and contorting the words already on your list—those below seek fresh inspiration from outside sources. These techniques ask you to look up from your complete list and find ideas elsewhere—in common expressions, pop culture, and past projects.

Search for Idioms, Quotations, and Song Lyrics

Look up text that contains words or concepts related to the brief. While these searches are likely to lead you to sentences and phrases—many of which will be far too long for a typical brand name—you may find useful ideas. Try shortening a phrase or using just part of it, so it's still recognizable but works well as a name. And even if this technique doesn't turn up any name candidates on its own, it may lead you to new, unexpected words and territories.

- *Float & Sting* (from Muhammad Ali's famous line)
- *White Light* (from a Velvet Underground song)
- *Capfeather* (from the expression, *a feather in your cap*)

Check Out Movies, Shows, Books, and Podcasts

Find media related to the topic at hand—at least loosely. Naming a brand of tea? Check out "How Tea Works," an episode of the podcast *Stuff You Should Know*. Naming a footwear company? Read *Shoe Dog*, by Nike founder Phil Knight. A tech startup? Good excuse to watch *The Social Network* or "Silicon Valley." Be ready to jot down ideas or thought starters while you're watching, reading, or listening. Throughout the name generation phase, immerse yourself in relevant content, either actively consuming it or simply letting it play in the background while you work.

- *Aloft* (learned about something called *winds aloft* while listening to a podcast about hot-air balloons)
- *MPH* (noted while re-watching Sandra Bullock and Keanu in *Speed*)
- *Samara* (joined the kids to watch Pixar's *Soul*; one scene features a whirlybird seed, technically known as a *samara*, fluttering to the ground)[6]

Take a Field Trip

Sometimes the inspiration you seek is not in a song or a book, but out in the world. Like a real field trip, this technique gets you away from your desk and forces you to immerse yourself in a relevant environment. Ask yourself: If you were teaching a unit on the topic at hand, where would you take the class on a field trip? We're naming a laptop, so we could visit a computer store or a technology museum. Naming a medical device? Visit the drugstore or a hospital. A pizza shop? Go to Little Italy.[7]

But field trip ideas don't have to be so literal. This is another opportunity to put the power of metaphor to use. If you're naming a cloud storage product, you could visit The Container Store in search of storage terminology. A cosmetics project could send you to the candy store or a farmers' market, depending on the product, the naming territories, and the desired tonality. Attempts to name a premium wristwatch could be informed by a trip to a premium car dealership—or vice versa.

---

[6] If *whirlybird seed* isn't ringing a bell, other nicknames for this seed include *helicopter seed, propeller seed, wing-nut, whirligig, polynose, spinner,* and *spinning jenny.*

[7] I'm assuming the real Italy is out of the question, but hey, if you've got the budget …

On the hunt for a few strong, fast, or lightweight ideas, I took a trip to my local hardware store. Here's what I found:

- **Impact** (from something called an *impact driver kit*, which sounds pretty tough)
- **Pureblue** (from a bluish Benjamin Moore paint color named *Innocence*, which made me think of having a weight lifted off one's shoulders; the word didn't feel quite right, though, so I looked up some synonyms and landed on *purity*)
- **Fuse** (from some time spent in the electrical aisle looking at circuit breakers and *fast-acting* fuses)

Mine Old Lists

This technique may be controversial, but I'm guessing every namer does it. Once you've worked on a handful of naming assignments, you're likely to start seeing naming briefs that look eerily familiar—you'll think, Didn't I see that naming territory recently? You may also find that names you've developed for one project work equally well—better, even—for others. By scouring old name lists, you can sometimes find unused ideas worth resurrecting. You may even want to create a *list of lists* full of rejected ideas from old projects, organized by theme or naming territory.

Looking through a couple of old lists, I dug up three suggestive, real-word gems:

- **Caliber** (suggests strength due to meaning of *high caliber* with respect to firearms)
- **Vector** (hints at speed via association with aeronautics)
- **Particle** (sounds like something lightweight)

Keep a List of Interesting Words

In addition to keeping lists from old projects, you may want to keep a list of words and phrases you find noteworthy. If you're a professional namer or know that you'll be working on many naming assignments in the future, jot down any interesting or favorite words as you make note of them, whether they come up in conversation, in a book, or simply pop into your head.

I recommend using a cloud-based file to store these words. That way, they're easily accessible from any phone or desktop, and you're unlikely to misplace the list, which you may open just once in a blue moon. Granted, these words may never make great names: since the only prerequisite for inclusion in the list is that you find them interesting, there's no reason to think you'll ever receive a naming brief for which they fit the bill. But I've put my list to use a handful of times, and you may occasionally find yourself in need of an off-the-wall idea. The words below, from my *Interesting Words* Google Doc, make sense for our brief.

- *Haymaker* (a fun slang term for a strong punch)
- *Quickdraw* (think fast)
- *Graphite* (it's lightweight)

New Angles of Attack

If you feel like you're beating your head against a wall, try going around it. Or scaling it. Or digging underneath. In other words, try an entirely different approach. The techniques below may take you out of your comfort zone—which happens to be exactly where some of the best brand names reside.

Employ Some Misdirection

As I mentioned in Chapter 6, although we're pursuing a new laptop name, the territories in our naming brief—*strong, fast,* and *light as a feather*—could work equally well for running shoes. What if we pretended we *were* naming shoes? That's the idea behind misdirection. Shoes for Usain Bolt would need to be lightweight but sturdy enough for an elite athlete. And the end goal, of course, would be speed. We could just as easily pretend to be naming a fighter jet or a moisturizing cream—one that feels light on your skin but is highly effective and works quickly.

This technique works best with a naming team, because the idea is to literally trick some members of the team by telling them they're naming something else. I've heard of large agencies drafting two versions of the brief—one that's accurate and another that replaces the *what we're naming* section with a fictional brand or product. It's a little harder to fool yourself, but misdirection can still serve as a useful thought exercise.

Playing out the running shoe thought experiment, I spent a few minutes on Usain Bolt's Wikipedia page and plucked out the three words below:

- *Bolt* (the perfect name for the greatest sprinter of all time— maybe it'll work for our product, too)
- *Sprint* (while we're thinking about sprinting ...)
- *Blur* (what Bolt looks like in some photos of him running)

Go Off-Brief

I've made a point of emphasizing the importance of the naming brief, and by no means should this suggestion be taken as a contradiction of that view. Sometimes, however, to get out of a rut or infuse some fresh thinking into a stale name generation phase, it pays to break the rules—at least temporarily. Try adding a new naming territory, allowing more leeway on the tonality, or even coming up with names that directly contradict the brief. Ultimately, if these names are truly off-brief, they should be rejected. But in the process of creating them, you may discover a new way of thinking about a naming territory, thereby uncovering a few unique, on-brief names.

For our hypothetical brief, I tried adding an entirely new territory— *thinness*—because it's a key selling point of the MacBook Air, our supposed competition. Who could forget Steve Jobs pulling the world's thinnest laptop from a manila envelope at his final Macworld keynote address? And since then, it's only gotten thinner—from 1.9 cm in 2008 to 1.6 cm in 2020.[8] So, while thinness is not a territory on our brief, let's explore it and see where we end up.

---

[8] Models released in 2018 and 2019 were only 1.5 cm high.

- *Plane* (We already have *Paper Plane* on the list, but I like the double entendre here—an airplane is fast, powerful, and defies gravity, while a two-dimensional surface is as thin as it gets)
- *Blade* (razor-thin, but also evokes a strong, sharp piece of metal capable of moving through the air quickly)
- *Lazer* (a thin beam of powerful light, fast and weightless, with a slight twist on the spelling)

Purposeful Distraction[9]

Many creative people find their best ideas bubble up from the subconscious only after they've stepped away from a project. Exercise, social interaction, and sleep can all serve this purpose—just be ready to capture any ideas in your notebook or smartphone.

Exercise

A growing body of scientific research suggests exercise can aid creativity. Wendy Suzuki, a neuroscientist and author of *Healthy Brain, Happy Life*, says that while more evidence is needed, early studies raise "the exciting possibility that exercise could make students more imaginative at school and adults more creative at work."[10] A study from the Stanford Graduate School of Education found that "creative thinking improves while a person is walking and shortly thereafter."[11] And more recently, a 2020

---

[9] The remaining techniques outlined in this chapter don't require examples; don't assume they're any less effective or important to the creative process.

[10] W.A. Suzuki. January 13, 2016. "A Neuroscientist Says There's a Powerful Benefit to Exercise That Is Rarely Discussed." *Quartz*, https://qz.com/592569/a-neuroscientist-says-theres-a-powerful-benefit-to-exercise-that-is-rarely-discussed/

[11] M. Oppezzo, D. L. Schwartz. 2014. "Give Your Ideas Some Legs: The Positive Effect of Walking on Creative Thinking." *Journal of Experimental Psychology: Learning, Memory, and Cognition* 40, no. 4, pp. 1142–1152.

paper in *Scientific Reports* "revealed that creativity … and everyday bodily movement [are] associated with each other."[12]

So, go for a walk. Get your blood flowing. Distract yourself. While working out, you may work out your naming challenge, too.

Socialize

A surefire way to distract yourself from the project is to become engrossed in a conversation about something else. Meet up with friends, go out to dinner, or simply walk around the office—to the proverbial water cooler, perhaps—and find someone to talk to. Discuss anything but the naming assignment. Just allow your mind to focus on other topics, pushing the name generation into the subconscious, where the creative magic happens.

"Pretty much anything that takes you completely away from what you're doing is really what you need," says Clive Chafer of Namebrand. "Going for a walk in the country, going for dinner with a friend—you'll get into conversation, and your subconscious still has the brief in it, and … you'll find yourself bringing your pad out at the dinner table. 'Excuse me a minute, can I just make a note? I just had an idea.' And they all think it's very fun. 'Oh, he's being creative again.'"

Sleep on It

According to a theory published by cognitive scientists in 2018, rapid eye movement (REM) sleep and non-REM sleep "facilitate creativity in different ways. … The iterative interleaving of REM and non-REM across a night boosts the formation of complex knowledge frameworks, and allows these frameworks to be restructured, thus facilitating creative thought."[13]

---

[12] C. Rominger, A. Fink, B. Weber, I. Papousek, and A. Schwerdtfeger. 2020. "Everyday Bodily Movement Is Associated With Creativity Independently From Active Positive Affect: A Bayesian Mediation Analysis Approach." *Scientific Reports* 10, no. 1, pp. 1–9.

[13] P. A. Lewis, G. Knoblich, and G. Poe. 2018. "How Memory Replay in Sleep Boosts Creative Problem-Solving." *Trends in Cognitive Sciences* 22, no. 6, pp. 491–503.

It's no surprise to me; I distinctly remember waking up as a kid—seven years old, maybe—and running to find paper and pencil so I could capture my idea for a new toy before it vanished from my half-awake mind. A few days later, I decided it was a silly idea for a toy—something that probably wasn't even physically possible, except in the mind of a seven-year-old. Too bad for me! My discarded idea was the Stomp Rocket, which is now a family-owned brand that's sold over 7 million toys worldwide. (*Stomp Rocket*, by the way, is a fantastic example of a descriptive name.[14])

Take a lesson from seven-year-old me—and from science—and keep a pad and pencil on your bedside table. Be ready to jot down names just before you drift off to sleep and as soon as you wake up in the morning. Don't let your Stomp Rocket take off without you.

Blockbusters

The previous chapter began with pulling names directly from the brief. From the path of least resistance, we've now arrived at the path of last resort—some extreme measures designed to bust through writer's block (in other words, *blockbusters*).

Try Some Bad Ideas

Despite our brainstorming rules (including *no criticism of ideas* and *go for large quantities of ideas*), some people—especially in a group setting—have trouble breaking through inhibitions and speaking up with ideas. If it's not good, people will start to question my creativity, they think. Even in a solo naming effort, this urge to self-filter can become a roadblock to progress.

Here's an idea from Eli Altman, Creative Director of the naming firm A Hundred Monkeys: To get past your inhibitions, try purposely coming up with stupid name ideas. What's the worst possible name for whatever you're naming? What would get you laughed at, scolded, fired, or sued?

---

[14] Although I suspect it has or will fall victim to *genericide* (see glossary and Chapter 14 for more on genericide).

The *bad ideas* exercise can loosen things up and take some pressure off name generation. It may work well as an icebreaker in a group naming brainstorm. As Eli puts it, "I think most people's approach to naming something, if they've never done it before, is just to sit at a table with a blank sheet of paper and a pen and wait until genius strikes them—which is a really frustrating and anxiety-provoking feeling. But coming up with bad names is fun and quick and easy."

And you never know—sometimes those bad ideas aren't so bad after all. Just think of names that could've been considered negative or scandalous, like *Virgin, Diesel, Acne Studios, Urban Decay,* or *Liquid Death.* And even if your bad ideas really *are* bad, they can lead to good ones. Eli Altman again: "Once you [come up with bad names], you have some fodder in front of you to look at and figure out, Well what makes these bad? And then if I know that, then if I flip that equation, what would make a name good?" What's the opposite of each of your bad ideas? What's wrong with them? Can your bad ideas help inform what kinds of names will work well?

Sprint

Sprinting, as a process or approach, originated in the world of software development. Appreciating the efficiency of hackathons and Scrum, designers of all stripes—from web design to product design—began incorporating *design sprints* into their processes. While many organizations have formal frameworks for design sprints (Google Ventures, for example, has published a recommended, five-day sprint[15]), the basic idea is as simple as it sounds: Come up with a bunch of ideas really quickly.

Shannon DeJong, founder of House of Who, recommends forcing oneself to complete simple, timed sprints as a way of breaking through writer's block. "Just do anything for 10 minutes," she says. "If you want to stop after that, ok, then maybe it's not the right time to do it. But most likely, you'll get into flow and you'll be on the treadmill

---

[15] J. Knapp. June 24, 2013. "How To Conduct Your Own Google Ventures Design Sprint." *Fast Company,* https://www.fastcompany.com/1672887/how-to-conduct-your-own-google-design-sprint

and it'll just—*fwip!*—and off you go. I think it's absolutely that way with creativity."

To perform a sprint, set a timer for 10 minutes. See how many ideas you can come up with before the timer goes off, regardless of quality. If you feel like you're just getting warmed up, keep going, or set a timer for another 10 minutes and begin again.

Like coming up with bad ideas, this technique takes the *quantity over quality* goal to an extreme and may result in a long list of terrible names. But it can also get you out of a rut, spark new thinking, and give you something tangible to reflect on, individually or with a group. What's wrong with the names you've hastily generated? What's *right* about them?

Mix It Up

My final piece of advice for busting through a creative block is to change something—your approach to collaboration, your tools, your surroundings—just about anything. I've mentioned the relative merits of solo name generation versus group brainstorming. Teamwork is great for exploring conceptual territories or when specialized knowledge is less important. But if the team's progress has stalled, make a change—break up the group and work individually for a while. If you've been on your own for some time and feel like you're at the end of your creative rope, maybe it's time to get back together with the group and bounce some ideas off each other.

While most name generation is inevitably augmented with online tools, it's often useful to step away from the computer and see what you can produce with nothing more than a notebook and a pen. There's something refreshing about going fully analog for an hour or two. At the very least, you'll give your eyes a break from the blue light of your screen.

And if you've been working in an office all day, try walking to a coffee shop or library. Or get some fresh air—why not move outside, to a nearby park or restaurant patio? Borrowing from the field trip technique, above, try finding a work setting that matches the mood of your project.

***

All the recommendations above, from obvious to obscure, deep to cheap, will help you start, build, and flesh out your complete list of name ideas. Feel free to try combining some of the ideas above: Listen to a relevant podcast while you're exercising or watch a relevant movie in a foreign language. As I've said, not every technique will be right for every project, but I encourage you to try each one on for size, see what works, and return to this list whenever you're in need of inspiration. Whatever you do, get creative—not just with your names but with your tactics.

Some Useful Tools to Start With

As mentioned throughout the steps above, a handful of reference books and websites can help you augment the complete list beyond your initial ideas. While a lengthier list is provided in Part IV, here are a few of the most useful tools for namers, with examples and brief explanations of each.

Dictionaries and Thesauruses

The most obvious tools for naming, a dictionary and a thesaurus, can help you find definitions, etymologies, and synonyms for ideas in the brief or names you've already generated. In addition to the standard reference books from Merriam-Webster or Roget's, consider some alternatives; a crossword puzzle dictionary organizes words by number of letters and includes useful trivia, while a Scrabble dictionary is limited to relatively short words (mostly eight-or-fewer letters long).

Online, sites like Dictionary.com, OneAcross.com (a crossword dictionary), Thesaurus.com, and Visual Thesaurus (visualthesaurus.com) can play similar roles to their physical counterparts, only faster. While the speed offered up by these sites is an obvious plus, don't underestimate the benefits of flipping through the pages of a good old-fashioned book. I once found myself searching online for a simple list of words in alphabetical order. It took me a few seconds to realize all I needed was a physical dictionary.

Word Combiners

To mix and match words or try different prefix and suffix combinations, search online for a keyword combiner like Kombinator (kombinator.org). These tools are designed to help with search engine optimization but can be helpful when compound and coined names are on the docket. A word combiner takes two or more lists of words or word parts as input, then outputs every possible combination from those lists. For example, imagine entering the following two lists into a word combiner:

List 1	List 2
• Pink • Black • Fire	• Berry • Rock • Stone

The combiner would produce a list of nine compounds (the length of your input lists multiplied together):

1. Pinkberry
2. Blackberry
3. Fireberry
4. Pinkrock
5. Blackrock
6. Firerock
7. Pinkstone
8. Blackstone
9. Firestone

Of course, I handpicked these words so that many of the resulting combinations would form well-known brand names (numbers 1, 2, 5, 8, and 9). In reality, this approach usually results in a long list of monstrosities with the possibility of a few beauties.

Language Dictionaries and Translation Sites

You may find additional name ideas in a language dictionary, like a Spanish-to-English or Zulu-to-English dictionary or phrasebook. Given the number of languages in the world, however, a site such as Google Translate can speed up the process of searching for translations of relevant terms. While you're exploring other languages online, you may want to check out a site like Forvo.com, which provides native pronunciations of foreign words.

Word Finders and Solvers

By allowing wildcards like *?* and * (for any single letter or string of letters, respectively), sites like OneLook (onelook.com) can help you find words that start with, end with, or contain specific letters. This can prove useful in a number of ways, including the following:

- Find real words and phrases that contain a short word you're exploring. For example, input *face** to find *facelift, faceplate,* and *face time.*
- Seek out opportunities to use rhymes, assonance (words that share vowels), consonance (words that share consonants), or alliteration. To find words that rhyme with *grub*, for example, try entering **ub* to see results like *hub* and *club*. For short words that might pair nicely with *pay*, enter *p??* to see *pad* and *pal.*
- Discover opportunities to create portmanteaus. Enter **oop** and **oup** to find words that might fuse well with *group*. Results such as *hoopla, nincompoop,* and *coupon,* might lead you to coined words like *groupla, nincomgroup,* and *groupon.*

Our Complete List So Far

Beginning in the previous chapter, we've now explored over 20 approaches to name generation, including creating mind maps around ideas from the brief, diving deeper with creative spelunking and research, and employing a handful of additional techniques to flesh out the list. The results, listed in Table 7.1, form a complete list of 100 names that fit our hypothetical brief.

You may not be impressed with the list so far—after all, naming is subjective, despite our efforts to make the process as objective as possible. Furthermore, at least two names on our list are identical to those of well-known competitor products: HP Elite *Dragonfly* and LG *Gram.* But remember, at this early stage in the process, our goal is *quantity.* By creating a long list, we'll eventually reach a very short list of high-quality, on-brief, available names. In the end, we only need one.

Table 7.1 List of 100 name ideas that fit the hypothetical brief

1. Aerostat	26. Dragonfly	51. Impact	76. Quickdraw
2. Aileron	27. Engine	52. Ironclad	77. Rocket
3. Alfa	28. Feather	53. Jet	78. Samara
4. Aloft	29. Fin	54. Lazer	79. Saturn
5. Alula	30. Float	55. Levitate	80. Scribble
6. Ammunition	31. Float & Sting	56. Light	81. Sketch
7. Antigravity	32. Floatable	57. Lightwing	82. Spacecraft
8. Arc	33. Floatflex	58. Missile	83. Spaceship
9. Arsenal	34. Fly	59. Mist	84. Sprint
10. Avimist	35. Flyology	60. MPH	85. Starfire
11. Avion	36. Fuse	61. Neon	86. Stoneskipper
12. Balloon	37. Fynn	62. Orbiter	87. Superfly
13. Bebop	38. Gesture	63. Osprey	88. Superman
14. Bellfeather	39. Glider	64. Ounce	89. Tempo
15. Blade	40. Gram	65. Oxy	90. Titanium
16. Blur	41. Graphite	66. Oxygen	91. Uku
17. Bolt	42. Harpoon	67. Paper Plane	92. Umoya
18. Boomerang	43. Hawkman	68. Particle	93. Vapor
19. Bullet	44. Haymaker	69. Pegasus	94. Vector
20. Bulletproof	45. Helium	70. Pictogram	95. White Light
21. Caliber	46. Housefly	71. Plane	96. Wildhorse
22. Capfeather	47. Hover	72. Plasma	97. Wing
23. Cubit	48. Hummingbird	73. Projectile	98. Wingamajig
24. Dart	49. Hydraulic	74. Propellant	99. Zeppelin
25. Dartbird	50. Hydrogen	75. Pureblue	100. Zoomerang

Review: Part II

Part II examined different ways of generating names, starting with the brief and going increasingly further afield in the pursuit of a long, complete list of ideas.

Chapter 4 zeroed in on the naming brief, which should be reviewed and approved by anyone with decision-making or veto power over the name. The brief typically includes some or all of the following information:

- A description of what's being named
- Ideas the name should convey
- Naming criteria (approach and construct)
- Desired tonality
- A description of the audience for the name
- A list of competitor names

Preparation for name generation starts with the creation of a complete list file, which tracks every name generated, keeps things organized, and automates some parts of the process. Getting set up also means identifying who will create names. While many organizations are tempted to crowdsource name ideas or host all-employee naming contests, these approaches often backfire. Instead, companies should select a small, core team of people tasked with generating the majority of name ideas. Members of this team can work individually, as naming is by and large a solo exercise, but they should meet regularly throughout the naming phase to compare notes and decide how best to divide and conquer.

Name generation typically begins with words pulled directly from the brief, followed by an exploration of related concepts through mind maps or similar tools. Other methods of spurring creative thinking, such as Edward de Bono's lateral thinking exercises and conceptual spelunking for parent, child, and sibling terms can help namers dive deeper and find unexpected ideas. Dictionaries, thesauruses, and a host of other websites and books prove immensely useful in applying these approaches and building out a name list. Most namers also search through encyclopedias and obscure reference materials, seeking further inspiration.

Chapter 7 detailed many additional techniques for fleshing out a name list, although not all will work well for every naming project. Combined, Chapters 6 and 7 suggest 20 ways to generate names. Using a mix of techniques like these, as appropriate for any given assignment, namers can easily generate a list of a hundred name ideas—a minimum for most naming projects.

Twenty Techniques for Name Generation

1. Start with the brief
2. Conceptual spelunking
3. Mix and match words or word parts to create novel compound names
4. Combine with common words and word parts
5. Lightly coin by altering spelling or adding, removing, or changing letters
6. Explore other languages
7. Look for rhymes or other forms of wordplay
8. Search for idioms, quotations, and song lyrics
9. Check out movies, shows, books, and podcasts
10. Take a field trip
11. Mine old lists
12. Keep a list of interesting words
13. Employ some misdirection
14. Go off-brief
15. Exercise
16. Socialize
17. Sleep on it
18. Try some bad ideas
19. Sprint
20. Mix it up—change your team dynamic, tools, surroundings, or something else

PART III

Narrowing Down to One

Perfection is achieved, not when there is nothing more to add, but when there is nothing left to take away.

—Antoine de Saint-Exupéry

CHAPTER 8

Shortlisting

Key Ideas

- Shortlisting has considerable impact on which names will be presented.
- When shortlisting, two to four namers typically review the brief, look at every name idea, and debate which ones to keep and reject.
- Awareness of common biases and blunders can help shortlisting teams keep an open mind and select name ideas with the potential for greatness.

Shortlisting is exactly what it sounds like: looking through the complete list of hundreds of names and selecting a few dozen to continue through the remainder of the naming process. It's a necessary step, because putting every name through trademark prescreening and linguistic searches would be time-consuming and expensive, not to mention unnecessary. Because of our *quality through quantity* ethos, we know full well that many of the names on our complete list—which should contain hundreds of ideas at this point, if not over a thousand—are not worth pursuing any further.

As simple as it may seem, this step shouldn't be taken lightly. By definition, shortlisting eliminates the majority of name ideas you've worked so hard to generate. In fact, successful shortlisting may be the difference between a good and bad outcome for the entire naming process. For someone overseeing a naming project involving a team of namers, this step is one of the most significant opportunities to exert influence over the final name. Great namers are not only capable of coming up with original ideas, but of plucking the potential diamonds from the rough.

To that end, I offer the following three pieces of advice, followed by three pitfalls to avoid when shortlisting.

Three Shortlisting Tips

Keep the Brief Handy

Even if you created the brief or are intimately familiar with it already, review it again just before shortlisting. As much as possible, memorize and internalize the brief so you can efficiently select and reject name ideas, keeping all the important criteria in your head. Refer to the brief as needed, however, throughout the shortlisting process, perhaps keeping it open on a separate monitor or printing a copy and leaving it on your desk.

Remind yourself of the *strategic* criteria the name should meet, so that you're not selecting ideas based purely on which ones grab your attention or sound good in your head (although, to be sure, these are both important criteria for successful brand names). You may also want the brief on hand for more immediate reasons, such as double-checking which words to avoid, which constructs are in and out of bounds, and what names are in use by competitors.

Meet, Discuss, and Decide

One typical approach to shortlisting is to organize a small meeting—two to four namers, say—and give each participant a copy of the complete list (as an on-screen document or printed copy[1]). After reviewing the brief together, meeting attendees silently pore over their copies of the complete list, a page or two at a time, circling or highlighting the strongest name ideas and making notes—rationale, questions, or new name ideas—in the margins. Stopping occasionally, participants take turns sharing their shortlisted names and rationale. When necessary, the group debates the merits of an idea. With input from everyone in the room, the list is finalized—either through consensus or executive fiat.

If an in-person meeting is impossible or inconvenient, another option is to create a shared spreadsheet with names listed in the left-most column. Each shortlister is assigned a column and leaves a *1* in rows

---

[1] But try to avoid printing, if possible, for the sake of the environment.

containing selected names.[2] This approach allows you to quickly tally up tick marks; names selected by everyone in the group probably don't require additional conversation, which can expedite the process.

That said, shortlisting shouldn't be driven by votes. Any name in question should be subjected to an open discussion or debate before moving to the next name. "I take a little set of index cards, and anything we like, we actually write it down and we put it on the table," says Jonathan Bell, Managing Director of Want Branding. "If someone disagrees, you just take it off the table." By giving the names a physical presence in the room, you'll ensure every remaining name is considered.

Don't Shortlist Alone

A scene in the Apple TV+ comedy *Ted Lasso* features a psychological phenomenon known as *semantic satiation*, in which a word temporarily loses its meaning after it's said out loud many times in a row. "Said 'plan' too many times. Word's lost all its meaning now," says the soccer coach. "Plan. Play-an? Plahn."

A similar affliction may impact you during shortlisting. When looking through page after page of names—many similar, some meaningless—portions of the list can seem to blur together, obscuring otherwise viable names. It's easy to lose your place or glaze over and miss a few ideas. By involving multiple people in the shortlisting process, you can reduce the chances of accidentally skipping over a winning name.

Another reason for multiple shortlisters is to encourage discussion and debate. Not only does this require the names be spoken out loud (which can influence how they're perceived), it also allows for a member of the group to advocate for an idea that others ignored or make a strong argument for shooting down a name that otherwise would've made the cut. With three people (or any odd number), you'll have the added benefit of a tiebreaker for ideas that divide the group.

Lastly, consider bringing in some outside naming experts to help you cull your list. Generally, it's fine to have the same people generate names and participate in shortlisting. But they may sometimes be too close to

---

[2] Ideally, avoid bias by obscuring participants' responses from each other.

the problem; fresh eyes could see value in a name they've overlooked. And even the most experienced and selfless namers can fall prey to bias when scanning a list that includes their ideas mixed in with those of other namers. I'm not sure what's harder: avoiding the bias toward picking one's own names or being sure not to overcompensate for that bias (i.e., avoiding picking one's own names even when they should make the short list). Outsiders—as long as they're experienced namers—can provide perspective and infuse fresh thinking into the process.

Three Shortlisting Pitfalls

Clients often make the three mistakes below when evaluating name ideas created by a namer or naming firm. As such, we'll revisit these when we talk about presenting names in Chapter 12. But even experienced namers can fall victim to the same hazards, either because they're unavoidable bits of human nature or because they're sometimes overlooked or forgotten.

Don't Fall in Love Too Soon

While shortlisting, you're sure to have some favorites. That's fine—but don't put too many eggs in any one basket. At this point in the process, you still don't know anything about whether these names are available or linguistically viable. Your favorite idea might be a competitor's trade name or mean *no go* in Spanish. So, maintain a healthy attitude of aloofness around your shortlisted names. It's an old namer's superstition that investing too much hope into one name will guarantee its downfall at the hands of the trademark gods.[3]

Don't Insist on Unanimous Approval

"I continue to believe the title leaves much to be desired," wrote Sid Sheinberg, president of Universal Pictures. "I would suggest we consider the title 'Space Man From Pluto.'" Luckily, the recipient of this memo,

---

[3] The same caveat applies to shortlisting many similar names. If all your names are similar, a single legal or linguistic concern can wipe out the whole list.

Steven Spielberg, was having none of it, and stuck with the original title of his film: *Back to the Future*.[4]

But not every team has a Spielberg—someone who'll stand his ground and prioritize instincts over consensus. Just think of all the reasons names like *Gap, iPad, Oracle,* and *Spanx* could've been shot down. At this point in the process, it's best to keep some risky ideas in the mix. There's plenty of time to get cold feet or allow some risk-averse executives to throw their weight around later on. If you start striking every name someone in the room feels "leaves much to be desired," you may be left with a short list full of space men from Pluto.

Don't Expect the Short List to be Obvious

Without a doubt, Nike is one of the strongest brands in the world. The name has quite a bit going for it, too: Nike is the Greek goddess of victory, a perfect association for a brand seeking to "bring inspiration and innovation to every athlete in the world."[5] Only four letters and two syllables long, with that nice *k* sound in the middle, it's certainly a step up from *Blue Ribbon Sports*, the forgettable name it replaced. And in retrospect, it seems like the obvious choice over other names the company considered, like *Bengal* and *Dimension Six*.

But it wasn't obvious. Phil Knight, founder and CEO, didn't care for it much at first. "I guess we'll go with the Nike thing for a while," he said, according to Kenny Moore, an Olympian and author of a book about Nike's origins.[6] "I don't like any of them," Knight continued, "but I guess that's the best of the bunch. Maybe it'll grow on us." Likewise, names that deserve to be shortlisted won't necessarily jump out at you. Like a fine wine, they'll probably need to breathe a little before you can tell how great they are. So, when shortlisting, you're not looking for greatness. You're looking for ideas with the *potential* for greatness—the names that may seem obvious in retrospect.

[4] I. Madison III. October 21, 2015. "A Truly Awful Alternate Title for *Back to the Future* Was Suggested by the Studio." *Vulture*. https://www.vulture.com/2015/10/back-to-the-future-awful-title.html

[5] Nike's mission, as listed on its website. https://about.nike.com/

[6] K. Moore. 2007. *Bowerman and the Men of Oregon*. Rodale Books.

CHAPTER 9

Trademark Prescreening

Key Ideas

- Conducting full legal searches on dozens of name ideas would be too costly and time-consuming; preliminary trademark screening is faster and less expensive.
- Professional trademark screeners are worth considering for their expertise, speed, and cost-effectiveness, but anyone can learn to conduct their own screening.
- The process for preliminary trademark screening can include checking the U.S. Federal trademark database and its counterparts outside the United States, searching online for identical and similar names, and visiting relevant domains.

Note: I'm not an attorney. This chapter is for informational purposes only. It should not be construed as legal advice for any individual matter, nor does it create an attorney-client relationship between you and me (the author) or the publisher. For further questions, I strongly recommend you speak to a licensed attorney who is familiar with trademark law.

***

Preliminary trademark screening, sometimes shortened to *prescreening* or referred to as a *knockout search*, is a standard step in the brand naming process. Or, at least, it should be. Even casual observers of branding loosely understand the risks of accidentally going to market with an unavailable name. They often oversimplify, however, thinking, You'll get sued for trademark infringement! and forgetting that many brands use identical names, although for different products or services (e.g., Dove soap versus Dove Chocolate).

Table 9.1 Many well-known brands use identical or similar names, but for different goods and services

Name	Famous brands
Apple	Apple (consumer electronics) Apple Records
Delta	Delta (airline) Delta Faucet Delta Dental
Domino/Domino's	Domino (magazine) Domino Sugar Domino's (pizza)
Dove	Dove (beauty products) Dove Chocolate
Eos	Volkswagen Eos Canon EOS (camera)
Finlandia	Finlandia (vodka) Finlandia Cheese
Graco	Graco (fluid management products) Graco (baby accessories)
Morningstar	Morningstar (financial services) MorningStar Farms (vegetarian foods)
Mustang	Ford Mustang Mustang Seeds
Pink	Thomas Pink Limited (AKA Pink Shirtmaker) Pink (Victoria's Secret sub-brand)
United	United (airline) United Van Lines

While just about anything *can* result in a lawsuit, more likely risks include the following:

- The U.S. Patent and Trademark Office (USPTO) might reject your trademark application, resulting in wasted time and money.
- Another company with a similar name might see your name, feel the need to protect their trademark, and send what's called a *cease-and-desist* letter (basically a note that says, Stop using that name, or we'll sue you).

- That company might *not* notice you're using a similar name— at least, not at first. Maybe far worse than receiving a cease and desist immediately is the possibility of receiving it years later. Imagine how expensive, time-consuming, and embarrassing it would be to have to change a name after years of investment.[1]

To avoid these pitfalls, namers (and their clients) should insist on legal searches as a critical step in brand naming. *Preliminary* trademark screening is built into most naming processes because asking lawyers to do a full legal search on a name can require too much time and money.

From a complete list of hundreds of name ideas, shortlisting might leave us with several dozen strong candidates. Rather than conducting full legal searches on all of them, namers subject the short list to faster, less costly searches. To conduct the preliminary trademark screening, a namer or prescreening expert (see below) pores through publicly available trademark databases and other sources to narrow the list of potential names by knocking out those with obvious legal challenges—those that are too similar to relevant, existing trademarks. Including the prescreening step ensures that only those names with a higher probability of success—those that a trademark attorney is more likely to deem usable after a deeper search—will continue through the naming process. Prescreening can also help prevent a worst-case scenario: having to return to a client or team, hat in hand, and deliver the news that the name everyone's fallen in love with is a legal quagmire.

Professional Preliminary Trademark Screeners

The easiest way to do preliminary trademark screening is to call for backup. That is, simply send your short list of name ideas to a professional trademark screening expert. As you'll see below, prescreening names takes *a lot* of time and patience. Furthermore, determining whether to reject

---

[1] A name change requires more than new business cards. Think about signage, a logo redesign, SEO, social media accounts, and more, not to mention rebuilding familiarity and trust with customers.

a name is rarely black and white, and the namer may be biased toward keeping a few favorite names on the list. For these reasons, and because outsourcing this step is surprisingly cost-effective, I prefer to rely on the expertise and experience of prescreening specialists.

Prescreeners such as Tessera Trademark Screening, Wilcox IP, and Litwin Kach's Trademarks and Branding Practice receive lists of name ideas—along with descriptions of what's being named and a few other details—and quickly assess the likely usability of each name. After scouring U.S. and other trademark databases, searching online, and checking dot-com domains, the prescreener will "score" each name. Names for which nothing similar is found for similar goods or services receive a positive score. When an identical or similar name is in use for similar goods and services, the name idea receives a less encouraging score. The prescreeners I've worked with can typically turn around a few dozen name ideas in 48 or 72 hours, and often for just a few thousand dollars.[2]

DIY Preliminary Trademark Screening

Still want to do it yourself? If you're only checking a handful of names or your budget is tight, you can learn a lot about the potential availability of your name ideas without any outside assistance. And, even if you're working with an expert, you'll benefit from a basic understanding of what they're doing. Below, I've listed steps anyone can take to run preliminary trademark checks on name ideas. Bear in mind, however, that any proposed brand name should undergo a full legal search by a trademark attorney before use.

Again, the goal of conducting a preliminary trademark search on a given name idea is to find out whether other companies are using an identical or similar mark for similar goods or services. The process can include the following steps:

---

[2] In addition to the number of ideas sent, factors that can impact pricing include where the name will be used, how many trademark classes must be searched, and requested turnaround time.

1. Check the U.S. Federal trademark database for identical names in all *international classes* (described below).
2. Check the U.S. Federal trademark database for *similar* names in international classes relevant to the goods and services of the project.
3. If applicable, screen trademark registers outside the United States for identical and near-identical names.
4. Search online for identical and similar names used for identical and similar goods and services.
5. Visit relevant domains for identical and similar use.

You can conduct these steps as *stage gates*, in that searches for each name can stop as soon as you find something sufficiently problematic to make continued searching unnecessary. In other words, if you find a significantly similar trademark for a competing product in the U.S. Federal trademark database (step one), no need to check foreign registers or do a Google search. To keep yourself organized, create a simple spreadsheet with name ideas on the left and a column for each step in your screening process.[3]

Searching the U.S. Federal Trademark Database

To search the U.S. Federal trademark database, use the USPTO's Trademark Electronic Search System or TESS. Access TESS by searching online for *uspto tess* or, at the time of this publication, by visiting uspto.gov/trademarks/search and clicking the *Search our trademark database (TESS)* button in the middle of the page.

- On the TESS home screen, shown in Figure 9.1, select *Basic Word Mark Search (New User)* to get started.
- To exclude dead and abandoned applications, select *Live* (leave the other options as they are).
- Type your query (see below) into the *Search Term* field.
- Press the *Submit Query* button.

---

[3] To download a free preliminary trademark screening tracker spreadsheet, visit brandnamingbook.com/downloads.

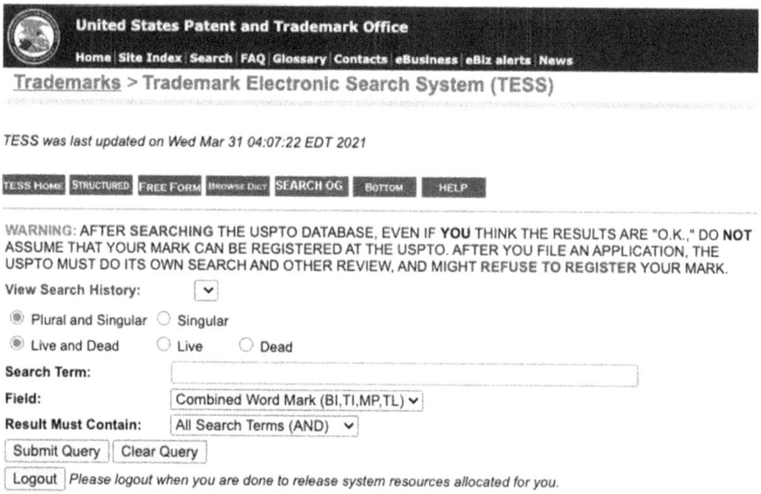

Figure 9.1 The Trademark Electronic Search System (TESS)

Depending on the project, your first query might be nothing more than a name idea. If the search returns any results from the database, you'll see a screen that displays the number of records found and lists the results. Above the list of results, you'll see a *Refine Search* field, where your query will have been replaced by something that looks a bit like code.

For example, let's say we're trying to come up with name ideas for a new, fruit-flavored candy. Our first query might be *Nektar* (one of our name ideas), in which case 14 records are returned (at the time of this writing) and the *Refine Search* field contains the following:

(live)[LD] AND (nektar)[COMB]

This code means you've searched TESS for live marks containing *nektar*. To narrow down the results, determine which *international classes* are most relevant for your project. International classes are a system used by the USPTO and other entities to classify every kind of good or service a business could provide—from legal services (class 042) to leather goods (018). The USPTO lists international classes on its website, but some of them are quite outdated, which can make it hard to tell which classes are applicable. An easy shortcut is to look up the registered trademarks of your (potential) competitors to see which classes they've registered in.

For our candy brand, we could look up Starburst and Haribo[4] and find they're registered in international class (IC) 30, among others. We can then refine our search by adding *AND (030)[IC]* in the *Refine Search* field to create the following query:

(live)[LD] AND (nektar)[COMB] AND (030)[IC]

Now, only one result comes up: Nektar Honey Crystals, described as *honey, granulated honey, and natural sweetener.* It's not fruit-flavored candy, but in my (non-lawyer) opinion, it's close enough for concern. Maybe you're thinking, But honey isn't the same as fruit-flavored candy. True, but put yourself in the shoes of that other company. Would you be upset if a candy company started using your brand name? Or imagine you're an avid consumer of Nektar Honey Crystals (whatever those are) and one day see Nektar brand candy at the grocery store. Might you draw a connection between the two? Avoid magical thinking here. Just because *you* know your product is nothing like theirs doesn't mean anyone else will jump to that conclusion.

Besides, had I continued, I would've soon found multiple candy brands using the name *Nectar*, and a slight variation in spelling probably isn't enough to avoid customer confusion. Regardless, had I not found any problematic *Nektar* or *Nectar* marks, I could have—and probably should have—expanded my search to include alternative spellings like *Neqtar* or *Nektr*. While I'm at it, maybe I should also expand the search to related goods and services, like soft drinks, just in case. And now you'll start to see how complex TESS searches can become. Take a look at the query below:

(live)[LD] AND (ne?t{V0:1}r)[COMB] AND ((030)[IC]
OR (032)[IC])

---

[4] *Starburst* is a great example of an abstract, real-word name. *Haribo* is an amalgam of the founder's name, Hans Riegel, plus the company's place of origin, Bonn (a German city).

The question mark in this query allows for any one character between *e* and *t*. The *V0:1* within curly brackets allows for up to one vowel—or nothing at all—between the *t* and *r*. That *OR* toward the end of the query ensures results from both the food class and the *Light beverages* class, which includes soft drinks. Another parameter that may come in handy is *[GS]*, which allows you to search by specific goods and services rather than broad industry classes. Swapping in *candy* for the international class field gives us the following query:

(live)[LD] AND (ne?t{V0:1}r)[COMB] AND (candy)[GS]

Having fun yet? The USPTO provides lengthy, additional instructions on how to search their database. If you're up for the challenge, have at it.

Remaining Steps

For name ideas that still appear relatively clean once you've searched the U.S. Federal trademark database, you can continue by looking at international equivalents—such as the Global Brand Database of the World Intellectual Property Organization (WIPO)—if relevant. Finally, try typing name ideas into a search engine, being sure to check alternative spellings, pairing the names with relevant keywords (e.g., *nektar candy*), and—as a final safeguard—checking the exact brand match dot-com domain (nektar.com).

Based on all your searches, assign each name a score to remind yourself whether you think the name is worth pursuing further. You can use *Go*, *Maybe*, or *Maybe not* (the preferred terminology of Tessera Trademark Screening), or try your own system: letter grades, high/medium/low, or maybe some traffic light color-coding. Once you've scored your name ideas, you'll have an even shorter short list—perhaps a list of *greens* and *yellows*—ready for the next step in your naming process: linguistic checks.

CHAPTER 10

Linguistic Checks

Key Ideas

- While some famous stories of supposedly disastrous brand names are inaccurate or exaggerated, careless naming can result in significant linguistic and cultural problems.
- Multilingual friends or colleagues—even if fluent in a language—won't necessarily know the latest slang, regional dialects, or local brands that could cause problems for a name.
- Professional linguistic checks reach out to multiple native linguists living in relevant countries and ask them about meanings, connotations, associations, and pronunciation challenges for each name.

Stop me if this story sounds familiar:

> When General Motors first launched the Chevrolet Nova, it barely sold in Mexico. Why? Because *Nova* translates to *doesn't go (no va)* in Spanish. With egg on their faces and marketing dollars down the drain, GM executives had to rename the car and start over in Spanish-speaking markets.

It's the most well-known tale of what namers call a *linguistic disaster*. And yet it's a tall tale—it never happened. According to Snopes,[1] a respected fact-checking site, "it's a wicked irony ... that the people who use this example are engaging in the very thing they're decrying, because a little

---

[1] And that's an interesting name, isn't it? Prior to creating the site, one of the founders used it as his username in online discussions. It's based on an unpleasant family of characters in some of William Faulkner's novels.

preparation and research would have informed them that it isn't true." Snopes claims the Nova sold well in Mexico and Venezuela in the 70s and that believing Spanish speakers wouldn't understand *Nova* is "akin to assuming that English speakers would spurn a dinette set sold under the name *Notable* because nobody wants a dinette set that doesn't include a table."[2]

Epic Fails and No Go Names

But the urban legend surrounding Chevy Nova isn't the only example of a linguistic disaster. If you're a fan of online listicles—or even if you aren't, frankly—you've probably seen one or two lists of so-called epic branding fails featuring photos of products with names like *Barf* (an Iranian dish detergent), *Pschitt* (a French soda), and *Sweat* (a Japanese sports drink), plus at least a dozen other names that evoke bodily functions or fluids. To English speakers, these names are hilarious, revolting, or both. But most of these products were never intended for English-speaking markets. When only sold in their home markets, these names make sense:

- *Barf* is Farsi for *snow*, a positive association for laundry detergent.
- *Pschitt* is named for the sound a soda bottle makes when opened.
- *Sweat* is used in the name of Pocari Sweat as an intentional reference to perspiration, because the drink claims to replenish "water and ions" your body loses while sweating.[3] The name doesn't seem to offend people in Asian countries where the drink is sold—most likely non-native English speakers, if they speak English at all.

---

[2] D. Mikkelson. April 03, 1999. "Did the Chevrolet Nova Fail to Sell in Spanish-Speaking Countries?" *Snopes.* https://www.snopes.com/fact-check/chevrolet-nova-name-spanish/

[3] I know, it sounds gross, but this drink is delicious.

If the Nova story doesn't go, and *Barf, Pschitt,* and *Sweat* aren't quite as bad as they sound, are there *any* real-world horror stories of brands with disastrous or embarrassing names? Oh yes, there are plenty.

In the 90s, Reebok recalled a women's athletic shoe named *Incubus*, admitting their mistake and saying they could not "imagine any responsible individual knowing what this name means and deciding that it's appropriate." What it means, according to Merriam-Webster, is "an evil spirit ... that has sexual intercourse with women while they are sleeping."

Another shoe, Zyklon, was renamed by maker Umbro because Zyklon B was the brand name of hydrocyanic acid used in Nazi death camps.

And a Fukushima-based refrigeration company recently backtracked on the English name of its cartoon mascot, *Fukuppy*, after realizing it was a colossal ... mistake.

Note that these branding facepalms need not involve translations or faraway lands. The *Incubus* name, for example, was presumably created for English speakers, by English speakers (albeit ones without access to a dictionary, it seems). That's one reason we often refer to these missteps as linguistic *or cultural* disasters—they can result from a name having a negative meaning in another language *or* from unintended, culture-dependent associations.

While a quick check on Google or in a dictionary can prevent some of the most obvious problems, how can any small team know how a word will be interpreted in multiple languages, countries, and cultures? The answer is simple, but maybe not as simple as you'd expect.

Don't Just Ask Your Multilingual Friends

Being multilingual might give you a leg up when generating names—maybe you can think of ways to convey ideas in several languages, instantaneously. But unfortunately, speaking multiple languages won't prevent you from creating a linguistically or culturally disastrous brand.

The same goes for having friends who speak Spanish, French, or Chinese. I can't tell you how many times I've had a client tell me they'll "just ask one of our engineers who speaks [insert language here]." I'm happy to see such linguistic, geographic, and cultural diversity within companies, but it's simply not enough of an insurance policy when you're talking about investing in a new brand name.

Unless you, your friends, or your colleagues are native speakers, live in the countries in question, and are trained linguists, you may miss something obvious. Consider this, for example: Some of my Chinese American friends speak fluent Mandarin, but they're unlikely to know the latest slang in Shanghai and Beijing, much less the names of local brands in those cities. And while I can easily reach out to a native Spanish speaker in Mexico City, I'm not confident his advice will apply in Spain, not to mention Spanish-speaking areas in the United States and around the world.

And what if you do get a resounding thumbs up or thumbs down on a name idea? Would you take one person's word for it, or would you want confirmation? No, don't just ask a few friends or colleagues—not on a decision this big. For a name you're planning to invest in and use for years, you'll need a professional opinion.

Invest in a Real Linguistic and Cultural Disaster Check

A professional linguistic and cultural disaster check—sometimes shortened to *linguistic check* or *linguistic search*—involves reaching out to multiple native linguists living in each relevant country.[4] Linguists are asked to answer at least three important questions about each name idea:

1. Does this name have any negative meanings or connotations in your language or culture?
2. Does this name have any associations (negative, neutral, or positive) in your culture or country—including any existing brands with identical or similar names?
3. Does this name have any pronunciation difficulties in your language?

---

[4] Ideally three linguists in each—or sometimes a larger odd number—to break ties in the event of differing reactions.

Professional linguistic checks can be conducted by naming agencies,[5] although they may simply outsource the work to a translation firm or specialist.

Translation firms like Transatlantic Translations Group (TTG), with whom I've worked many times, can easily survey native linguists in countries and languages around the world. Send them a list of names and a list of languages, and a few days later they'll return a raw report with verbatim input from respondents:

- "This name is a bit difficult for a native Bengali speaker to pronounce."
- "This sounds similar to the name of a high-end supermarket chain in Hong Kong."
- "Negative connotations: phonetically similar to 屍 [si1] in Cantonese, meaning *corpse; carcass.*"

Obtaining a report like this is a quick, cost-effective way to prevent linguistic disasters. For example, a review of 30 names in eight languages can cost less than $1,000 and take less than 24 hours.

But interpreting the results of such a report requires some experience. Should you throw out an otherwise great name because one person in India found it hard to pronounce? How should you interpret responses from three Russian linguists, one who reports a name idea is terribly offensive and two others who simply respond, *Ok.* For a deeper appreciation of the relative risk tied to names in the report, you may want to seek the expertise of someone like Laurel Sutton, who co-founded the naming firm Catchword and now runs a business dedicated to thorough linguistic checks with in-depth reports.

I go through all of the material, look at what people say, follow up with them if I need to—if there's an unclear answer or if there's violent disagreement between two people where someone says, This is great, and the other person says it's terrible. ... I need to get a better feel for

---

[5] See list of select naming agencies in Part IV.

what that means. I put it in a report that a client can easily digest ...
that says, Out of those 20 names, here are the ones that I think you
should proceed with.

—Laurel Sutton, Founder & Linguist, Sutton Strategy

While it's no fun learning that one of your favorite name ideas is Spanish
slang for *wanker*—as is Mitsubishi's *Pajero* SUV, in an apparently true
alternative to the Chevy Nova story[6]—linguistic checks are often one
of the most fascinating steps in the naming process. If you're interested
in language, as most namers are, this is where you'll learn about which
consonant clusters are tongue twisters in some languages, how tonal
languages such as Mandarin and Cantonese interpret a single morpheme
in many different ways, and that words composed of alternating
consonants and vowels (e.g., *Toca Boca*) are easy to pronounce in most of
the world's languages.

---

[6] J. Hudson. October 26, 2011. "Nokia's 'Prostitute' Phone Joins Ranks of
Bungled Brand Names." *The Atlantic.*

CHAPTER 11

What About the Domain?

Key Ideas

- Availability of an exact brand match dot-com domain should not drive the naming process.
- Solving for the brand name first, then the domain, increases the likelihood of landing on a good name with the desired meaning and tonality.
- When obtaining the desired web address is impossible or cost prohibitive, teams should consider alternative solutions, such as adding a descriptor to the name or using a dot-co or dot-net domain.

A 1999 episode of *Saturday Night Live* featured one of their famous fake ads, in which Chris Parnell deadpans straight to the camera: "A lot of investment companies rushed onto the Internet, but Dillon/Edwards took their time. Sure, when they were ready, there was only one web address left, but it's one you can count on." Then a pair of announcers take over, as the actor types on his home computer. "For mutual funds ... clownpenis dot-fart."[1]

Like a lot of comedy, the genius of the joke is that it's rooted in truth—even back in 1999, it felt like all the desirable dot-com domains were already taken. Maybe that's why, if you read through any list of tips for naming your company, one piece of advice—almost without fail—will revolve around ensuring the domain name is available. For example, the fourth of "12 Tips

---

[1] The writers at *Saturday Night Live* wisely used an apparent founders' name for this fictional bank to suggest an old, trustworthy brand in an often-stodgy industry. Meanwhile, *Saturday Night Live* is another descriptive name, so long that it's often shortened to an initialism: *SNL*.

For Naming Your Startup Business" in *Forbes* is "Get the .com domain name."[2] (This advice comes from an executive at a venture capital fund that invests in companies with names like *Phreesia* and *Opzoon*.)

A recent *Ad Age* article about brand names advises readers to "make sure the name is available" by running "a Google search along with a social media check."[3] Going a bit further than the *Forbes* article, an *Ad Age* panelist suggests the name isn't important at all, so long as the dot-com is obtainable: "Don't stress on the name itself; make sure you can claim your digital real estate first."

Focusing on the Dot-Com Is Bad Advice

Despite these recommendations to the contrary, the conventional wisdom among naming experts is that a *dot-com first* approach to naming rarely ends well. When the *Ad Age* article was published, professional namers derided it on social media. Chief among their complaints was the suggestion that domain availability should outweigh name quality.[4]

For decades, namers have downplayed the importance of domain availability, pointing out that many successful companies have launched without exact brand match dot-coms. Furthermore, modern Internet users are more likely to search for brands using keywords than try to guess

---

[2] R. Harroch. "12 Tips For Naming Your Startup Business." *Forbes*. October 23, 2016.

[3] "Stumped on Your Business Name? 8 Tips for Choosing the Right One." *Ad Age*, June 26, 2020.

[4] If it's so off-base, why does the *dot-com first* advice keep showing up in perennial *tips for naming* articles? I suspect there are three reasons: (a) Owning an exact brand match dot-com was once more important—both because it made companies easier to find and because it came with considerable cachet. Most people don't name companies very often and are likely to have an outdated view of domain names (i.e., old habits die hard). (b) Most professional namers have at least a rudimentary understanding of trademark law; without this understanding, nonexperts are likely to conflate domain availability with legal availability. The two are barely related. (c) Nonexperts are recycling old ideas. Called upon to say something useful about naming, they're likely searching through outdated blog posts and parroting incorrect information.

a brand's online address. Today, these arguments hold—if anything, they become more persuasive every day:

- More and more brands—even well-funded start-ups and established companies—are forced to use imperfect domain names; popular, newer brands.
- Peloton and Away use onepeloton.com and awaytravel.com, respectively, and Nissan—one of the world's most valuable brands—never owned nissan.com. (Instead, find them at choosenissan.com.)
- Google's Chrome browser was the first to combine the address bar with the search bar (something they call the *omnibox*). Other browsers have followed suit, making it even easier to rely on search terms rather than an exact URL (short for universal resource locator, the technical name for a web address).
- Early on, the Internet had seven top-level domains (TLDs), and most businesses used one of three: dot-com, dot-net, or dot-org. As of this writing, a new website could have any one of over 1,500 TLDs—and the list is growing.

Solve for the Brand Name First, Then the Domain

Another argument against prioritizing an exact brand match dot-com domain is that determining whether a URL is obtainable—and at what price—can prove difficult and time-consuming. Sites like GoDaddy do offer bulk domain searches, which can instantly tell you which of many domains are available for about $11.99. But what about those that are *parked*, meaning they're registered but not in use? Or domains that point to long-defunct websites? What if they're for sale, too, but for $100? No bulk search tool can reveal this information instantly, especially when finding the true price of a domain may require multiple rounds of negotiation. If you insist on an exact dot-com, you're either stuck with a readily available, inexpensive domain (Opzoon.com, anyone?) or the prospect of contacting dozens of domain owners to gauge prices and availability.

That's why the naming process favored by most professional namers solves for the name first, then the domain. As detailed in Part II, namers create hundreds of ideas and subject the strongest candidates to a battery of rapid screenings, including preliminary trademark searches and linguistic checks. Screening typically includes a visit to [name].com, but names aren't ruled out simply because someone owns or uses a domain.[5] Once a decision-making team whittles the long list down to a handful of preferred ideas, it's time to dig into the domain question.

Solving for the name first ensures the brand name conveys the desired meaning and personality, among other attributes of strong names. The reverse approach—finding an available dot-com first—still requires legal availability checks (because owning a domain doesn't give the owner trademark rights) and linguistic checks. It also may result in an ugly, hard-to-spell, or hard-to-pronounce name and could lead to a tenuous, post-rationalized story to link the name to the brand.

But the Dot-Com Is Taken—Now What?

These days, it seems the exact dot-com for any pronounceable string of letters—not to mention every real word—is owned. Therefore, brand names derived through the naming process described above usually don't come with freely available dot-com domains. In this situation, resourceful companies can take many paths from name to domain. Here are some possible next steps, using the (purely illustrative) newname.com domain as an example:

First, Dig Deeper to Find Out Whether the Domain Is for Sale

Just because a domain search doesn't show newname.com as available doesn't mean the owner won't sell. Don't visit newname.com repeatedly,

---

[5] The only obvious reason to strike a name based on what appears at [name].com is finding that it's an identically or similarly named brand of similar goods and services (in other words, a legal concern). That said, I've killed names upon finding large, well-known brands using the domain; even if they operate in an entirely different category, they could cause marketing and SEO challenges. And once, I had a client reject a name because [name].com housed a leather fetish retailer. They just couldn't bear the thought of a customer accidentally winding up on that site.

as this may trigger a price increase. The safest way to learn more is to work through a third party—preferably a professional domain broker—to find out whether the owner is open to selling and get a sense of the potential selling price. If you do contact the owner directly, be careful what you reveal. If the owner suspects a company with deep pockets is interested in the domain, you'll wind up overpaying for it.

Add a Descriptor

Often, the most straightforward solution for the domain is adding a descriptive word after the brand name. For example, Dove, the popular American chocolate brand, owns dovechocolate.com, not dove.com. (The latter is owned by the personal care brand of the same name.) Before purchasing tesla.com in 2016, Tesla could be found at teslamotors.com. Descriptors can speak to what a company does (newnametaxprep.com), what it sells (newnamecoffee.com), where it's located (newnamesf.com), or any other pertinent information related to the company (e.g., newname-global.com or newnameinc.com). Select a handful of acceptable descriptors, append them to your name ideas, and go back to the bulk domain search tool mentioned above.

Add Words to Create a Phrase

Many new brands solve the dot-com challenge by creating phrases that contain their names. Dropbox originally occupied getdropbox.com (but acquired dropbox.com in 2009). Recess, a sparkling cannabidiol (CBD) beverage, owns takearecess.com. See whether your name works well in a familiar or natural-sounding phrase, starting with a dictionary of idioms or a tool like OneLook.[6] Looking at some names from the hypothetical naming project featured in Part II, *Plane* could live at planeasday.com. *Neon* might become justlikeneon.com, borrowed from some John Mayer song lyrics. Words to consider in front of just about any brand name include *choose*, *get*, and *we are*. For a longer list of ideas, see Table 11.1.

---

[6] Described in Chapter 7.

Table 11.1 Words to add to a brand name when seeking a domain

Before the name	After the name
get[name].com	[name][**descriptor**].com
weare[name].com	[name]**hq**.com
thisis[name].com	[name]**online**.com
the[name].com	[name]**global**.com
my[name].com	[name]**store**.com
try[name].com	[name]**inc**.com
choose[name].com	[name]**app**.com

Consider Alternative TLDs

Dot-com still reigns supreme in the land of TLDs, and maybe it always will. Nonetheless, many companies opt for dot-net. Slideshare and Box, for example, were first located at slideshare.net and box.net. Start-ups and gaming companies frequently use dot-co or dot-io domains (*I/O* is short-hand for *input/output*, which has relevance in software development and some technical fields). Check the availability (or sale price) of newname.co and newname.io to join start-ups like Hinge (at hinge.co) and Datrium (at datrium.io).

Depending on the nature of your business, descriptive TLDs like dot-store or dot-consulting may be relevant. Consider Twitch, the streaming platform for gamers: It remained at twitch.tv until after its 2014 acquisition by Amazon. Now, twitch.com redirects to twitch.tv.

Explore Domain Hacks and Other Creative Solutions

In the early 2000s, sites such as Blo.gs and Delicious (found at del.icio.us) pioneered the use of *domain hacks*—the creative use of domain extensions to create names and words. Domain hacks have given rise to a handful of naming fads, including a slew of *ly* names, like Zenly (zen.ly) and Parsely (parse.ly), which rely on the country code top-level domain (ccTLD) of Libya. The *ly* has arguably jumped the shark, but domain hacks can still work as long as they're solving the domain challenge for a selected name, rather than driving the naming decision in their own right.

Downsides of domain hacks include potential impacts on search engine optimization (SEO) and risks associated with attaching your site to the ccTLD of a politically unstable country. Other creative domain solutions may work better, depending on the name in question. When Alphabet launched in 2015, the media swiftly—almost gleefully—reported that BMW owns alphabet.com.[7] But as you'd expect of Google, they were one step ahead: Alphabet Inc.'s URL is abc.xyz.

Combine Any of the Above

If needed, try different combinations of the ideas above. For example, a radio station that fails to obtain newname.com could explore options like newnameradio.fm (a descriptor and an alternative TLD), tunetonewna .me (a phrase and a domain hack), or newnamerad.io (a descriptor and a domain hack). Similarly, a tax preparer could consider taxesbynewname .co, getnewname.tax, or newnametax.es.

A Great Name Is Worth More Than a Lousy Name With a Perfect Domain

Whatever you do, don't let domain availability drive the naming process. While the tactics above may lead to a viable domain solution, they should only be contemplated once ideas have been derived through a naming process rooted in brand strategy and prioritizing the meaning, tonality, and other qualities of the brand name (including legal availability).

Consider the major brands mentioned above. No matter your opinion of names like Tesla and Slideshare, they are easier to spell, pronounce, and remember than the tortured alternatives that might have resulted from an insistence on exact brand match domains. Imagine: We could be shopping for cars at Tezzly.com and watching slide presentations at Slydshr.com.[8] Maybe some venture capitalists would've looked more favorably on their exact dot-com domains, but I'm glad these companies didn't base their naming decisions on a list of tips in *Forbes*.

---

[7] F. Lardinois. "Google Is Now Alphabet, But It Doesn't Own Alphabet.com." *TechCrunch*. August 10, 2015. https://techcrunch.com/2015/08/10/google-is-now-alphabet-but-it-doesnt-own-alphabet-com/

[8] Purely illustrative (and terrible) ideas.

Table 11.2 Famous brands and start-ups that launched with and/or still use imperfect domains

Company/ brand	Original/ current domain	Notes
Alphabet (Google)	abc.xyz	Alphabet.com is owned and in use by a subsidiary of BMW.
Away (luggage)	awaytravel.com	Away.com is owned and in use by Orbitz (online travel company).
Basecamp	basecamphq.com	Founded in 1999; acquired basecamp.com in 2012 (basecamphq.com now redirects to basecamp.com)
Box	box.net	Founded in 2005; acquired box.com in 2011 (box.net now redirects to box.com)
Dropbox	getdropbox.com	Founded in 2007; acquired dropbox.com in 2009 (getdropbox.com now redirects to dropbox.com)
Hinge (dating app)	hinge.co	Hinge.com redirects to homepage of SOSS, a "door hardware" company.
Intermix (apparel)	intermixonline. com	Intermix.com is not in use.
Method Products	methodhome.com	Method.com is in use by a global design firm.
Nissan	choosenissan.com and nissanusa.com	Nissan.com is owned by a computer company in North Carolina.
Peloton	onepeloton.com	Peloton.com belongs to a "drilling and well data software" company.
Recess (CBD beverage)	takearecess.com	Recess.com is not in use.
Slideshare	slideshare.net	Slideshare.com now redirects to slideshare.net.
SoulCycle	soul-cycle.com	Soulcycle.com is in use by a BMX shop in Amsterdam.
Square	squareup.com	Founded in 2009; acquired square.com in late 2011 or early 2012 (square.com now redirects to squareup.com)
Tesla	teslamotors.com	Founded in 2003; acquired tesla.com in 2016 (teslamotors.com is no longer in use)
Tile (tracking devices)	thetileapp.com	Founded in 2012; acquired tile.com in 2017 (tile.com now redirects to thetileapp.com)
Twitch	twitch.tv	Founded in 2007; acquired twitch.com sometime after 2014 acquisition by Amazon (twitch.com now redirects to twitch.tv)
Zoom	zoom.us	Founded in 2011; acquired zoom.com in 2018 (zoom.com now redirects to zoom.us)

CHAPTER 12

Presenting Names

Key Ideas

- Getting a diverse team to agree on a brand name has more to do with psychology than creativity.
- The naming presentation helps drive alignment by addressing many foreseeable challenges of evaluating and selecting names in a group setting.
- Everything from the number of names, order of names, visuals shared along with each name, and more should be taken into careful consideration when presenting, as these details can influence how the names are perceived.

Getting a client (or your own team, for that matter) to agree on a single brand name is 1 percent creativity, 99 percent psychology. Maybe that's an overstatement, but for all the effort that goes into creating names, much of the work of naming is in getting a group of people—often with diverse roles, backgrounds, or levels of comfort with creative exercises—to select a final name.

That's where the naming presentation comes in. And it's why a good naming presentation is not just about showcasing the best ideas, but also driving consensus and buy-in. Managing disparate reactions and opinions is a messy business, but a well-crafted presentation can mitigate many predictable challenges of consensus-building.

How to Structure a Naming Presentation

One reason to insist on a formal presentation of names is that it lends some gravitas to the naming process and helps ensure the audience is paying attention. Rather than e-mailing name ideas or listing them on a whiteboard and asking people to vote, build a presentation in slide software such as PowerPoint, Keynote, or Google Slides. In addition to standard content—title slide, agenda, next steps—the naming presentation should contain the following five sections:

1. Overview
2. Review of the naming brief
3. Priming the audience
4. Name ideas
5. Summary of name ideas

Let's examine each section in more detail.

Overview

Start by reminding the decision-making team that the purpose of the meeting is to select a handful of preferred name candidates—not to decide on a final name. (This reminder sets the right expectations and takes some pressure off the meeting.) They can't narrow it down to one at this point in the process, because name ideas will have only undergone preliminary trademark searches. A more in-depth legal search should inform the final decision. Because that deeper search can nix several names, plan on sending five or six to the attorneys.

Sharing a process overview at this point can also serve as a subtle reminder of how much work has gone into the names you're about to share—that these are not just a selection of your favorite, off-the-cuff ideas, but name candidates derived through a rigorous process.

Review of the Naming Brief

Even if the audience helped create or has recently read and approved the naming brief, it's best to review it again immediately before assessing names. Remind everyone what served as jumping-off points for naming, what was explored and avoided, and any other relevant details from the brief.

Priming the Audience[1]

The next section of the presentation aims to put meeting attendees in the right frame of mind for reviewing names. One by one, counter some of the common misconceptions of naming that could derail the presentation. Slides in this section often include the following reminders:

- The strongest brand names are grounded in strategy. Decision makers should ask themselves which names will work, not which name they like the most. Good names are also stretchable enough to support future growth, easy to remember, and legally and linguistically viable (among other qualities listed in Chapter 1).
- The name is just one part of the brand. Avoid the temptation to make the name say everything, since it will likely be viewed or heard in the context of a visual identity, messaging, or other brand elements. This point can be demonstrated by showing a name that looks like nothing more than a word on a slide until other brand elements—a logo, a package, a website—are added.
- Keep an open mind. Consider names like *Caterpillar* or *Starbucks,* which initially must have felt silly, controversial, or otherwise problematic. Suppress knee-jerk reactions at this stage—the best name ideas can feel off-putting at first.
- Don't expect a name to *jump off the page.* Names are rarely love at first sight. Even if one decision maker favors a name immediately, chances are the rest of the team won't feel the same way.
- The lawyers will have to review names before you start using one (i.e., you're not walking out of this meeting with a final name).
- Some naming presentations include a slide highlighting the total number of names generated. If you're presenting 20, your complete list may contain 500. Like the process overview above,

---

[1] To be clear, I am not suggesting you use "Priming the Audience" as the heading for this section in your presentation. I usually title it something like "About Brand Names" or "Thoughts on Evaluating Names."

this information hints at the hard work behind the names. On the other hand, sharing these numbers might lead attendees to request access to the complete list, which is best avoided.

Before sharing names, I recommend telling the audience you'll present all the ideas first, then invite discussion. This approach is more efficient and encourages evaluation of the names as a group, rather than one at a time. By assessing the full list at once, attendees can more easily consider which names will work best from a strategic standpoint, as opposed to looking at each idea in isolation and asking themselves, Do I like this name?

Name Ideas

The right number of names to present depends on what types of names you've explored, whether you'll be doing multiple rounds of naming, and other project-specific details. But try to find the sweet spot: Present too few, and the audience will feel your exploration didn't go far enough. Worse, you'll have lowered the probability that one or more of your ideas will resonate. On the other hand, if you present too many names, the decision-making team may be overwhelmed and suffer from paralysis by analysis. In a typical, first-round naming presentation, I like to share 20–30 name ideas.

As shown in Figure 12.1, create a slide for each name based on a simple template that includes:

- The name, near the center of the slide, in a large, neutral font
- Optionally, a handful of bullet points at the bottom of the slide (smaller text) with rationale, strengths of the idea, relevant definitions, or illustrative marketing copy
- A visual aid—a simple mockup showing the name in a realistic context to help the audience make the necessary mental leap to envision the idea as a brand name

To avoid biasing decision makers, make the visual aid virtually identical on each slide (although you may want to alternate between two similar designs so viewers don't become blind to the mockups). If you're naming a company, a business card can work well—a neutral, grayscale design with a handful of realistic details like the company's address and a ® next to the name. If you're working on a product name, a mock package or web page could work. Do not create a unique visual identity or mockup for each name—you need not be a psychology expert to see the inherent risk in doing so: Does the CEO hate that name idea, or does she just hate orange?

As you present each slide, say the name out loud. It's important that the audience hear the ideas, too, to confirm pronunciation, aid in recall, and imagine the name in an audio-only context (as they would over the phone or in a radio ad). Next, make a case for the name—explain where the idea came from, why you think it's interesting, why you like it, or anything else significant. Your goal shouldn't be to hard-sell the name, but to ensure your audience has a well-rounded understanding of the idea and time to process it fully before moving to the next slide.

A brief note on the order of the names: While I try not to overthink it, I do try to (a) get any expected ideas out of the way first (e.g., any listed in the brief or suggested in previous meetings), (b) put very similar names next to each other (as *variations on a theme*), and (c) given the primacy and recency effects—cognitive biases that result in people remembering the items at the beginning and end of lists better than those in the middle— err on the side of putting stronger candidates closer to the beginning and the end of the presentation.

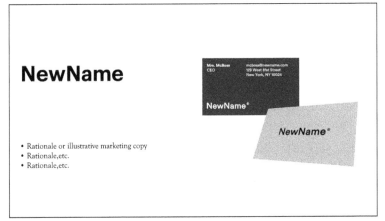

Figure 12.1 A typical name slide from a naming presentation

Summary Slide

Immediately following the individual name slides, show an alphabetical list of every name from the presentation, all on one slide.

Instructions for Feedback

Now comes the moment of truth. Assuming attendees have refrained from sharing their opinions during the presentation, this is your first opportunity to hear what's resonating. The success or failure of the entire meeting may hinge on the next few words uttered. For example, imagine this worst-case scenario: The CEO blurts out, "I don't like any of these." If no one's brave enough to contradict the boss, the meeting is over, and you'll have trouble regaining the team's confidence.[2]

Of course, if you've done your homework, a swift dismissal of all the names is unlikely. More likely reactions at the end of a naming presentation include, "We definitely can't use that one" or "I think we can all agree these three won't work." Faced with a tough decision, it's natural to pursue a simple, process-of-elimination strategy. But as soon as a negative thought is attached to a name, it creates a chilling effect—anyone who liked the idea is less likely to speak up. If you let everyone snipe at their least favorite names—even for ridiculous reasons—they'll decimate your list before you can say *Boaty McBoatface.*

To avoid this fate, I recommend being somewhat dictatorial in your instructions. Here's an example of what I might say as soon as the summary slide appears on the screen:

> Here are the 25 names I just presented, in alphabetical order. I want to get your feedback now, but I need you to follow one rule: Please start by sharing only your positive reactions.
>
> With this many names, you probably saw a few you think can't work. That's ok—it's part of the process. But keep any negative thoughts to yourself, for now, to avoid biasing everyone else. Even

---

[2] Giving leaders a preview of the naming presentation can also help avoid this fate.

if we ultimately reject a name, we need to know what people like about it because it may spark another idea.

These instructions create the opposite of a chilling effect (a warming effect?). Instead of a single "I don't like it" poisoning the whole discussion, positive reactions will spread contagiously throughout the group. Those who were too shy to advocate for an idea will be more likely to do so. Your audience may even pile on, eager to share what they love about a name that's starting to look like a crowd favorite.

As meeting attendees list the names they feel good about, keep a private tally. Once everyone has had a chance to speak, share some thoughts on which ideas the team is rallying around. These names are frontrunners for full legal searches. If the project calls for an additional round of naming, selected names may also inform future name generation.

After the Presentation

One final thought about naming presentations: While it's standard business practice to send out a slide deck after presenting, avoid sending it to anyone who didn't attend the meeting, and remind recipients to keep it to themselves. E-mailing a naming presentation (or worse yet, pasting names into an e-mail) deprives the names of necessary contextualization. Having read this chapter, you already understand the importance of putting name ideas in context—priming the audience, reviewing the brief, and managing the discussion. Without the presentation, you may have a list of creative ideas, but you're missing that other 99 percent.

In Summary: Dos and Don'ts

My recommendations aren't one-size-fits-all; I encourage you to experiment and find what works best for you when presenting names. But much of my advice stems from trial and error—I've made plenty of mistakes and watched other branding professionals bomb like standup comics on off nights. To avoid that fate, bear in mind the following list of dos and don'ts for naming presentations:

Do...	Don't...
1. Remember the presentation is about more than good ideas—it's about driving consensus and buy-in.	1. Assume naming is simple—that you'll solve it in one late-night brainstorm session over pizza and beer.
2. Give a formal presentation rather than e-mailing name ideas or listing them on a whiteboard and asking people to vote.	2. E-mail name ideas around and/or ask a team to vote for their favorites on a list.
3. Remind attendees how much work has gone into the names by reviewing the process to date and (optionally) sharing the total number of names created.	3. Share the complete list of every name that's been generated so far.
4. Review the brief again immediately before names are assessed.	4. Stop on each name and invite discussion as you're presenting—instead, present every idea, then discuss all of them.
5. Prime the audience with content that counters common misconceptions of naming (e.g., that the right name will magically jump off the page).	5. Try to create a unique visual identity or mockup for each name.
6. Create a slide for each idea with the name in a large, neutral font, bullet points of rationale (optional), and a visual aid.	6. Try to hard-sell a name—if the decision makers have a strong negative reaction, it's probably easier to move on.
7. Say each name out loud and explain the thinking behind the name or why you think it's interesting.	7. Let attendees start sharing negative feedback before positive—instead, give them specific instructions to start with positive reactions only.
8. Carefully consider the order of the names—without overthinking it.	8. Send the deck to decision makers or influencers who did not attend the meeting. (The context is important.)

CHAPTER 13

Full Legal and Final Selection

Key Ideas

- After one or more rounds of naming, decision makers select a handful of names for full legal searches, which are performed by experienced trademark attorneys.
- The final name should be selected by one or two senior leaders or a slightly larger group; insisting on broad consensus means prioritizing a lack of offensiveness over other qualities, such as memorability and distinctiveness.
- Name research—when done correctly—and scorecards can help simplify difficult naming decisions.

Ideally, after all the work that's gone into creating, screening, and presenting a few dozen names, the decision-making team eagerly embraces five or six ideas. But it's not always so easy. If the team can't agree or only one or two names make the cut, it may be time to conduct a second round by repeating steps two through five of the naming process: generating, shortlisting, screening, and presenting new name ideas.

Unless the brief has changed, round two usually produces fewer, more focused options—variations on a theme from round one, perhaps. Second-round names can either augment or form the entire batch that ultimately goes to the lawyers. Or sometimes, additional rounds simply reinforce the team's confidence in their first-round picks. Even after a successful first round, a second round of naming can help everyone feel they've left no stone unturned.

No matter how many rounds it takes, after the naming presentation, it's time to select a handful of names to go into full legal.

Full Legal Searches

Looks like it's time to call your lawyer. In an ideal scenario, the trademark attorney receives somewhere between three and six name candidates, assesses them, and finds that—in their expert opinion—one or more names is relatively ownable or safe to use (although lawyers are unlikely to use those words). The decision-making team can simply wait to hear back, then decide on a final name based on the legal opinion and any other factors they've prioritized.

Full legal searches can take anywhere from a few days to a few weeks. It's a good idea to find an experienced trademark attorney in advance and have a conversation about your naming project, when you will likely have ideas to send, and any deadlines you're facing for a final naming decision. Despite the fact that they may have to deliver some bad news about a name you were hoping to use, I've found it's best to treat lawyers as partners in the naming process rather than adversaries.

Another way to speed things up—and save some money, potentially—is to rank the names in your list and ask your lawyer to search them one at a time. If your top choice isn't too risky to use, move forward with that name and forget about the rest of the list. If the lawyers recommend against it, move on to your next choice, and repeat.[1]

Making the Decision

The best way to choose the final name depends heavily on the decision-making team's structure and culture. Can the CEO or VP of Marketing review options, listen to input, then settle on a name singlehandedly? Maybe the three co-founders can discuss behind closed doors and reach an agreement? The best names tend to come from decisive leaders who feel empowered to make bold choices.

---

[1] Don't expect a clear yes or no from your lawyer. The riskiness of using any name is almost always a gray area, and you're looking for clarity on the different shades of gray—the relative risks (or lack thereof) associated with different name candidates.

Some organizations, however, demand a greater degree of alignment among the team. It's wise to seek input from a diverse set of colleagues, but consensus can also dilute creativity. As the cliché goes, if everyone has to agree on the pizza, you'll wind up with plain cheese—innocuous but inert. But most of the great brand names stand out, demand attention, and generate buzz—even if they're not for everyone. More mushroom-and-anchovy than Margherita. (Or more Vietnamese coffee than vanilla, to use the ice cream version of this adage.)

An insistence on unanimity can also stall the project indefinitely. When teams get stuck at this final decision point, I recommend a simple list of pros and cons for each name. In some cases, a detailed *scorecard* can help. And in the most extreme cases of indecision, a more drastic measure may be called for: name research.

Scorecards

A scorecard is a simple table in which each row contains a name option with notes about legal availability, feedback from the linguistic check, domain options, and any other factors that could influence the final decision. Based on a review of each row's information and in consideration of project priorities, names are ranked or given letter grades. While the final name won't necessarily be the one with an A+, the scorecard can help break down the decision and make it feel less daunting.

For illustrative purposes only, here are a few rows from a scorecard, filled in with fabricated information:

Rating	Name	Strategic rationale	Linguistic checks	Legal risk	Domain availability
A	Folkways	Ways of living, thinking, acting	Potential pronunciation difficulties in French	Low	Folkways.com for sale—price TBD
B+	Jack of Hearts	Honor + empathy	No concerns	Medium	JackofHearts.co for sale for approx. $5k–$15k
C	Quence	Coined, abstract (quince, quench)	May have negative connotations in Cantonese	Medium	Dot-com owned, but not in use; broker trying to make contact

Name Research

In the previous chapter, I advised against seeking opinions from people who haven't been involved throughout the naming process. Unfortunately, conducting primary research on name ideas means doing precisely that. However, regardless of whether respondents like or even understand the name ideas, research can provide valuable insights when done right. Here are three tips:

1. Don't ask respondents whether they like the names. Instead, tie every question to an attribute or tonality you're hoping the final name will express. For example, you could ask how *powerful* each name sounds or whether names have a *graceful, flowing* sound.

2. At the end of the survey or conversation, ask everyone to share every name they can remember. While other questions ask people to describe their perceptions,[2] this question tests recall directly. It's far from a perfect measurement, but it can provide useful estimates of each name's memorability. (To remove some bias, randomize the order of the names before sharing them with respondents.)

3. Evaluate reactions to the names relative to each other, not in absolute terms. Be prepared for your name ideas to receive lukewarm or negative reactions—this is normal, and you can usually take it with a grain of salt. (Remember, you're asking people to react to unfamiliar ideas without much context.) Let's say 40 percent of respondents agree that *Brontos* sounds powerful versus 20 percent for *Della*. The key finding would be that twice as many people thought the first name sounded powerful, not the fact that neither topped 50 percent.

---

[2] Something we're surprisingly bad at, as illustrated by the psychology study about car speed from Chapter 1 (Loftus and Palmer 1974).

CHAPTER 14

Securing and Launching the New Name

> ## Key Ideas
>
> - The final name should be secured through trademark protection (if applicable) and acquiring or creating a domain, among other possible steps.
> - When launching the new name, teams should prepare a clear, concise explanation of the name, plan every detail of the launch in advance, and release everything at once, if possible (e.g., the name, logo, website, ad campaign).
> - Successful brand launches require teams to commit to the name and avoid backtracking in the face of (inevitable) pushback from some observers.

After all the work you've done to land on a final name, you'll want to lock it down, protect it, and ensure a smooth brand launch. The best way to do so can vary significantly depending on your goals, what you're naming, and where you are in the world. While these steps aren't usually considered part of the naming process, they play a vital role in the eventual success or failure of the name.

Secure Your Brand Name

Typical steps for securing the name include applying for a trademark and getting your domain name and social media handles squared away. If you're naming a company, you may also need to register the legal entity name and a *doing business as* name (DBA).

Apply for a Trademark

The best-known way to protect a brand name is to apply for a trademark. You can do this directly with the U.S. Patent and Trademark Office (USPTO) or a local equivalent, or have a lawyer do it on your behalf. As mentioned previously, I'm not an attorney and can't give legal advice. That said, anyone creating a brand name should at least understand some basic principles:

1. It's *trademark* protection you're looking for, not *copyright* protection. The latter is primarily intended to protect the rights of creators like authors, playwrights, songwriters, and artists.

2. A service mark (SM) is like a trademark (TM) but for services rather than goods.

3. If you want, use the ™ or ˢᴹ symbol to indicate you've applied for a trademark—or intend to—but haven't yet secured it. Switch to ® once your trademark is registered.

4. Not every name needs to be trademarked. The iPhone boasts a *dual-camera system*, and while I'm confident a fair bit of thought went into that phrase, I doubt Apple has tried to register a trademark for it. Overly descriptive names can't be trademarked, but they still have a role to play in clearly explaining a product and its features to customers.

5. Once you secure a registered trademark, protect it. Keep an eye open for other companies using an identical or similar name for related goods or services. If you discover a transgressor, notify them of your registered trademark or contact your lawyer.

6. Be sure to renew your trademark registration by filing any necessary maintenance documents (e.g., five years after the original registration date with the USPTO). Worst case, failure to effectively maintain a trademark registration can result in *genericide*—the loss of legal protection due to widespread use of a mark as the generic term for a product or service. Many words we now use every day were initially trademarked brand names, including aspirin (still a trademark in many countries outside the United States), dry ice, escalator, hovercraft, kerosene, and zipper.

Get the Domain and Social Media Handles

If you haven't already, it's time to buy or create the URL for your brand. For a new company, that probably means buying a dot-com, dot-net, dot-co, or dot-io. A nonprofit or educational institution may warrant a dot-org or dot-edu, respectively. And if you're naming a product or service, you may want to add a subdirectory to your company website rather than buying an entirely new domain. For example, the online home of Samsung's Galaxy Z Flip smartphone is samsung.com/galaxy-z-flip, not galaxy-z-flip.com.

Assuming your brand will have a social media presence, secure your handles on platforms like Twitter, Instagram, Facebook, LinkedIn, and YouTube. Even if you have no intention of using these sites at launch, it's best to reserve a username in advance. If possible, using the same handle across all social media platforms—one that's identical or similar to your web domain, ideally—will simplify your marketing and make it easier for users to find you. Try a username search tool like KnowEm (knowem.com) or Namechk (namechk.com) to look into the availability of different usernames across many platforms at once.

Register Your Legal Entity Name and Doing Business As Name

If you're naming a company, you may need to register your *legal entity name* with your local government. In many parts of the United States, for example, businesses must be registered at the state level. Note that the legal entity name need not match the brand name. Don't make the mistake of thinking that another business having registered an identical name in your state automatically precludes you from using that name. Many companies have brand names that differ from their entity names. While Starbucks famously dropped "Coffee" from its brand name, the legal entity is still Starbucks Coffee Company. And the legal entity for Subway, the sandwich chain, is—strangely—Doctor's Associates Inc.

In the United States, a DBA (also known as a *fictitious business name*) allows this separation between a company's legal entity name and its brand name. If your legal entity name is different from the final brand name you've selected, look into registering a DBA with your city, county, or state.

Launch

It's finally time to release your name into the wild! Advice for planning and executing a successful brand launch could fill an entire book. When it comes to the brand name specifically, it's essential to get your story straight, tell it well, and stick to it.

Get Your Story Straight

Draft a clear, simple, and concise explanation of the name. If it's replacing an old name—a company rebrand, for example—be sure to include rationale for the name change; the switch should coincide with any substantive changes in the business to avoid the appearance of a change for change's sake.

Remember, you are not the audience for this explanation—put yourself in the shoes of a customer and think about how the story will sit with them. Ensure anyone who'll be communicating about the name, from employees to agency partners, knows and understands the rationale behind the name.

Tell It Well

Create a detailed plan for the launch, including where and when the name will show up. When it goes public, the name should be supported by other verbal and visual identity elements. That might mean creating a tagline, an *about us* section for the website, or boilerplate language for the bottom of a press release, as well as a logo or full-scale ad campaign. Don't announce the name in a press release followed by a brand launch six weeks later. Don't launch the website one week and the social media campaign the next. Do it all at once.

Think carefully about the order in which audiences learn about the name. Plan on sharing the name inside your organization first so that employees are familiar with it well in advance of having to answer any questions from customers or the media. (But don't be too surprised if an internal-only launch leaks to the public.) You may want to give your most important customers or partners a heads up, as well.

Stick to It

On August 10, 2015, Google announced the creation of Alphabet, its new holding company. Later that day, I noticed a tweet from Eric Schmidt, Google's former CEO:

> *I think the Alphabet name is Awesome.*
> —Eric Schmidt, Twitter post, August 10, 2015, 2:44 p.m.

I can't say for sure whether Schmidt, then executive chairman, planned his note to coincide with the launch, but I'd be willing to bet he did. Presenting a united front of immediate, coordinated, positive messaging around the name is one way to mitigate negative reactions to a new name—and virtually every new name (or name change) will receive its fair share of negative reactions, even if it's not as high-profile as Alphabet. When telling employees, key customers, and partners about the name before it launches publicly, you can also recruit them as cheerleaders for the name on the day of the launch.

Finally, stick to your guns. The name you're launching is the expression of an agreed-upon brand strategy. It has survived preliminary trademark screening, linguistics checks, a full legal search, and everything else you've thrown at it. Out of hundreds of contestants, it's your finalist. Don't let a case of cold feet undo all that work. From rejected logos to abandoned package designs, the clearest indicator of a failed brand launch is backtracking.

***

It may take weeks or even months for your new brand name to feel natural in conversation. But, with a great name and a well-executed brand launch, it always gets there. Remember, we see thousands of brand names every day, rarely stopping to think about where they come from or what they mean. Our minds are malleable enough to accept coffee from a *Moby Dick* character and shoes from a Greek goddess. Your name will become second nature soon enough.

That's not to say you shouldn't put effort into finding the *right* name, of course—a word or two that inspires or informs, giving you a head start against the competition. A meaningful, memorable name that strikes a balance between strategic, creative, and technical qualities. That's not trendy, tortuous, or too clever by half. Find the right name, and you're on your way to building a brand that not only stands out—but stands the test of time.

Review: Part III

Part III walked through the steps required to get to a single, final name from a complete list of hundreds of ideas.

Shortlisting culls the complete list down to a few dozen that will continue through preliminary trademark screening and linguistic checks. Despite its seeming simplicity, the importance of getting the short list right should not be underestimated. Namers involved in shortlisting must avoid becoming overly committed to any favorite ideas, treating shortlisting as a mere voting exercise, or expecting the short list to jump off the page.

Shortlisted names must then clear a series of hurdles before they're presented, beginning with preliminary trademark screening and linguistic checks. Preliminary trademark screening—a fast, inexpensive way to avoid obvious legal problems—should always be included in the naming process. Anyone can screen name ideas using publicly available information, but this step is often outsourced to professional trademark screeners who can reliably and efficiently screen dozens of names at a time.

To prevent linguistic or cultural missteps like Reebok's *Incubus* shoe and Mitsubishi's *Pajero* SUV, namers rely on professional linguistic checks, not the opinions of multilingual friends or colleagues. A professional check reaches out to multiple native linguists living in relevant countries and asks them about meanings, connotations, associations, and pronunciation challenges for each name.

While names with obvious legal problems or linguistic challenges can be dropped, those without an available, perfect domain—in other words, [brandname].com—shouldn't be rejected out of hand. This point of view runs counter to advice found in many articles and blog posts on naming, but many famous brands have successfully launched and grown without exact brand match dot-coms. Furthermore, Internet users are likely to use search engines to find what they're looking for rather than typing a URL into an address bar.

Insisting on an exact brand match dot-com domain may push companies toward misspelled or meaningless names. Instead, most namers recommend solving for the brand name first. Companies can then attempt to acquire a desired dot-com or consider alternatives paths to an acceptable domain, such as adding a descriptor or other words to the brand name, trying alternative top-level domains (e.g., dot-net or dot-co), or exploring domain hacks and other creative solutions.

Names that survive preliminary trademark screening and linguistic checks may be shared in a naming presentation, a critical tool in driving alignment around a final name. At multiple points throughout the presentation, meeting attendees are told what to expect, reminded of the work that's gone into the names they're seeing, and given instructions on how to provide constructive feedback.

Following the presentation, decision makers usually send five or six name ideas to a trademark attorney for full legal searches. With input from the lawyers, the final name is selected. Scorecards and name research can help with a difficult naming decision, but research needs to be handled very carefully and taken with a grain of salt, as people tend to react negatively to new ideas, especially when shown out of context.

The selected name is often secured through some combination of trademark protection, acquisition or creation of a domain and social media handles, and, in some cases, registration of a legal entity name and *doing business as* name (DBA). Launching a new brand name—once it's been secured—requires careful planning and preparation. At launch, the new name should be explained clearly, concisely, and with the support of any other new brand elements such as a logo, website, or ad campaign. While new brand names often feel awkward at first and may have to win over a leery public, their success requires steadfast commitment. Over time, brand names start to feel natural—obvious, even, in retrospect.

PART IV

Resources

He came up with the names. They were good times.
            —Colson Whitehead, *Apex Hides the Hurt*

The Namer's Bookshelf

It's fun to imagine a professional namer sitting in a room full of obscure dictionaries, out-of-print thesauruses, and dusty tomes full of Greek Mythology or esoteric industry jargon. While sites like Wikipedia and Thesaurus.com are fast and free, physical books sometimes have advantages in terms of authority, organization of information, and detail. (Not to mention the lack of blue light.) Beyond your standard dictionary and thesaurus, the books below may prove useful.

Dictionaries

- *Flip Dictionary* by Barbara Ann Kipfer
- *The Describer's Dictionary: A Treasury of Terms and Literary Quotations* by David Grambs and Ellen Levine
- *The Official SCRABBLE Players Dictionary* by Merriam-Webster

Other Books for Naming Research

- *Bartlett's Familiar Quotations* by John Bartlett
- *Brewer's Dictionary of Phrase and Fable* by Dr. Ebenezer Cobham Brewer
- *The Dictionary of Imaginary Places* by Alberto Manguel and Gianni Guadalupi
- *English Synonymes Explained in Alphabetical Order with Copius Illustrations and Examples Drawn from the Best Writers* by George Crabb
- *Random House Word Menu* by Stephen Glazier
- *The Secret Language of Symbols* by David Fontana

Books About the Origins of Brand Names

- *From Altoids to Zima: The Surprising Stories Behind 125 Famous Brand Names* by Evan Morris
- *Why Did They Name It...?* by Hannah Campbell
- *Wordcraft: The Art of Turning Little Words into Big Business* by Alex Frankel

Books About Writing and Language

- *Dreyer's English: An Utterly Correct Guide to Clarity and Style* by Benjamin Dreyer
- *The Elements of Style* by William Strunk Jr. and E. B. White
- *The Mother Tongue: English And How It Got That Way* by Bill Bryson

The Namer's Browser Bookmarks

Beyond printed resources, namers are increasingly turning to online tools, which provide efficiencies and capabilities that books alone can't. Many of the sites listed below were recommended by professional namers I interviewed on season one of my podcast, *How Brands Are Built*.[1]

Dictionaries and Thesauruses

- Dictionary.com
- The Free Dictionary's Idioms dictionary (idioms.thefreedictionary.com)
- One Across (oneacross.com)
- Online Etymology Dictionary (etymonline.com)
- Visual Thesaurus (visualthesaurus.com)
- WordHippo (wordhippo.com)

Word Combiners

- Kombinator (kombinator.org)
- WordsMerger (wordsmerger.com)

Language Dictionaries and Translation Sites

- Forvo (forvo.com)
- Google Translate (translate.google.com)

---

[1] Find a list of season-one guests in the Acknowledgements at the beginning of the book.

Word Finders, Solvers, and Other Useful Sites

- English-Corpora.org
- OneLook (onelook.com)
- RhymeZone (rhymezone.com)
- USPTO Trademark Electronic Search System (tmsearch.uspto.gov)
- WordNet Search (wordnetweb.princeton.edu)
- Wordnik (wordnik.com)

Select Naming Firms
(and Related Companies)

Agencies That Specialize in Naming

- A Hundred Monkeys
- Catchword
- House of Who
- Igor
- Lexicon
- Namebase
- NameStormers
- The Naming Group
- Operative Words
- Pollywog
- PS212
- River + Wolf
- Tanj
- Tungsten
- Want Branding
- Zinzin

Full-Service Branding Firms That Provide Naming Services

- Character
- Finien
- FutureBrand
- Interbrand
- Landor
- Lippincott
- Matchstic
- Pentagram
- Red Antler
- Siegel+Gale
- Wolff Olins

Glossary of Naming Terms

abbreviation
Any *brand name* formed by the shortening or contraction of a word or phrase, including *acronyms, amalgam names,* and *initialisms*

abstract name
A *brand name* with no apparent connection to the underlying brand

acronym
A *brand name* formed from the initial letters (or groups of letters) of a longer name or phrase and pronounced as a word; Examples: ASICS, Fiat, GEICO, Nabisco, NASA, Qantas

allonym
In linguistics, a coordinate or sibling concept; For example, two ideas that share a *hypernym* (parent concept or category)—as *red* and *green* share the hypernym *color*—are allonyms

alphabetism
See *initialism*

alphanumeric name
A *brand name* formed from the combination of letters and numerals

amalgam name
A *brand name* formed from the first few letters of each word of a longer name; Example: Nabisco (from *National Biscuit Company*)

arbitrary name
A real-word, abstract *brand name*—a real word with no apparent connection to the underlying brand; Example: Quartz (a news organization)

associative name
See *suggestive name*

brand name
One or more words used to identify a brand

cacography
A deliberate misspelling, often silly or comical; Examples: Froot Loops, Krispy Kreme, Playskool

camel caps/case	See *internal capitalization*
clipping	See *truncated name*
coined name	A *brand name* that is entirely invented or contains newly invented words
complete list file	A dedicated computer file (e.g., a spreadsheet or document) used to store and keep track of every name idea generated for a project
composite name	See *compound name*
compound name	A *brand name* formed by connecting two or more real words, in their entirety, to form a new word; Examples: Zipcar, Fitbit, PayPal
deconstructed name	See *truncated name*
descriptive name	A *brand name* that clearly describes what it refers to (e.g., a feature, product, service, or organization)
domain name	A name used as an Internet address, including a second-level domain (typically relates to a company or brand name) and a top-level domain or domain extension (e.g., com, net, or org) separated by a dot (.)
domain hack	The creative use of a domain extension to create a word or name out of a *domain name*; Examples: blo.gs, del.icio.us, parse.ly
double-barrel name	See *compound name*
empty vessel name	A *coined name* that is also an *abstract name*—invented words without prior definitions, into which meaning can be poured; Examples: Exxon, Kodak, Dasani
eponym	A *brand name* that is also the name of a person (or personified creature), whether that person is real or fictitious and whether or not they have anything to do with the brand; Examples: Aunt Jemima, Chuck E. Cheese, Louis Vuitton, Tesla

evocative name	See *suggestive name*
exact brand match (EBM)	
dot-com	A *domain name* consisting of a brand's name followed by *.com,* without any modifiers or descriptors; Examples: warbyparker.com, patagonia.com
fabricated name	See *coined name*
fanciful name	See *empty vessel name*
founder's name	A *brand name* based on the name of the brand's founder(s) or creator(s); Examples: Twinings Tea, McDonald's, Disney (Note: A founder's name is a *descriptive name* and a kind of *eponym*)
full clearance search	See *full legal search*
full legal search	An in-depth assessment of legal availability and risk associated with name ideas, conducted by an experienced trademark attorney
fused name	See *compound name*
genericide	A loss of trademark rights due in part to a *brand name* being used interchangeably with the generic term for its associated product; Examples: dry ice, escalator, hovercraft, kerosene, and zipper were initially trademarked brand names
geographic name	A *brand name* based on the brand's place of origin; Examples: Hudson's Bay Company, Bank of Taiwan, Nantucket Nectars, New York Life, Mystic Pizza (Note: A geographic name is a kind of *descriptive name*)
hypernym	In linguistics, a parent concept or category; For example, *bread* is a hypernym of *sourdough* and *rye* because sourdough and rye are types of bread

hyponym	In linguistics, a child concept or subordinate; For example, *spoon* and *fork* are hyponyms of *utensil* because they are types of utensils
initialism	A *brand name* formed from the initial letters of a longer name or phrase and pronounced letter by letter; Examples: AT&T, CNN, IBM, KFC
internal capitalization	The use of a capital letter in the middle of a name to signal separation between parts of the name; Examples: BlackBerry, PayPal
invented name	See *coined name*
knockout search	See *preliminary trademark screening*
legal name	The official name of a business or other entity, as registered with the government and written into official documents like articles of incorporation
linguistic/cultural disaster check	An assessment conducted to avoid significant difficulties arising from *brand names* with pronunciation challenges or problematic meanings, connotations, or associations in relevant languages or cultures
magic spell name	See *misspelled name*
master list	See *complete list file*
medial capital	The capital letter(s) in the middle of a name that employs *internal capitalization*
merged name	See *compound name*
metonym	The name of one thing used as the name of some other, related thing; Examples: Crunch (a gym), The Coffee Bean & Tea Leaf

mimetics	A word or speech sound that mimics another word or sound; Examples: Ping (mimics the sound of a putter hitting a golf ball), Incogmeato (sounds like *incognito*), 可口可乐 (the Chinese brand name for Coca-Cola, pronounced *kĕkŏukĕlè*)
misspelled name	A *brand name* that employs *cacography*
morpheme	A meaningful unit of language (i.e., a word or word part) that can't be divided into smaller meaningful units
naming approach	How a *brand name* connects to qualities or ideas related to the underlying brand (e.g., *descriptive names, suggestive names, abstract names*)
naming brief	A short document that outlines objectives and parameters for the *brand name* to be developed
naming construct	How a *brand name* is structured (e.g., *real-word names, coined names, compound names*)
naming spectrum	See *naming approach*
neologism	See *coined name*
portmanteau	A new word formed by combining the sounds and meanings of two existing words;[1] Examples include: Clamato, Jazzercise, Nespresso, Verizon
preliminary trademark screening	Assessing name ideas by reviewing *trademark* databases and other sources and removing from consideration those names with obvious or likely legal challenges

[1] A portmanteau is also a piece of luggage with two compartments. This meaning of the word was first suggested by Humpty Dumpty in Lewis Carroll's *Through the Looking-Glass.*

real-word name	A *brand name* made up of one or more real, correctly spelled words in the primary language of the brand and its audience
shortlisting	The process of selecting a subset of name ideas from the *complete list* to continue through the remainder of the naming process, including *preliminary trademark screening* and *linguistic/cultural disaster checks*
simplex	See *compound name*
sound symbolism	The theory that speech sounds have intrinsic meaning
suggestive name	A *brand name* that evokes a quality of the underlying brand
synecdoche	A type of *metonym* in which something is named after one of its parts (e.g., a restaurant named *Table*) or a part is named after the whole (e.g., a toaster named *Kitchen*)
synonym	A word with the same meaning as another word
tonality	The feeling a *brand name* evokes
trademark	A word, phrase, or symbol that identifies the source of the goods or services as distinct from those of others
truncated name	A *brand name* formed by removing one or more parts of a real word; Examples: Cisco (from *San Francisco*), Leidos (from *kaleidoscope*)
uniform resource locator (URL)	The technical term for an Internet address, including the protocol (e.g., http) and the *domain name*
word combination	See *compound name*
wordmark	All or part of a logo featuring the *brand name* written in a distinctive, standardized typographical treatment

Naming Brief Template

Project Overview

- Add overarching objective, details about timing, and other background information.

What We're Naming

- Write a simple explanation of the product or company to be named/renamed.
- If helpful, include images and links.

Description of Target Audience

- Provide a description of the people who will be seeing/using this name.
- If relevant, include details such as demographics, roles or titles, and likely state of mind when encountering the brand name.

Ideas the Name Should Convey

- List three to five big ideas for names to try to convey.
- Ideas can be concrete (e.g., *coffeeshop*) or abstract (e.g., *spirit of community*).
- For each idea, provide any additional explanation, context, and/or relevant words/name ideas.

Naming Approach and Construct

- Circle the area(s) to explore on the graphic below (Figure 19.1).
- List any other details related to the name structure (e.g., *must be preceded by parent brand name* or *will likely be followed by Gaming*).

Figure 19.1 Well-known brand names organized by naming approach and naming construct

Name Tonality

- List adjectives to describe the appropriate tonality/personality for the name.
- Identify any tonalities to avoid (e.g., *nothing too technical-sounding*).

Competitor/Peer Names

- List brand names this name will be seen alongside, including competitors, partners, or vendors.
- If possible, include notes on which names decision makers like or dislike, and why.

Explore and Avoid (Optional)

- List any words, word parts, concepts, or name ideas to explore or avoid.

Explore	Avoid

Previously Explored/Rejected Names (Optional)

- List names already considered, along with an explanation of why they are/were liked and why they were ultimately rejected (if they were).

Brand Names for Inspiration (Optional)

- List any other brand names (in or out of category) the decision makers like, and why.

Screening/Domain Requirements (Optional)

- Detail any preliminary trademark screening criteria (e.g., which international classes to screen against).
- Provide any linguistic/cultural disaster check criteria (e.g., which countries/languages to review).

- Describe any domain name requirements or objectives (e.g., hoping for an exact dot-com but willing to add *we are* before name to secure a dot-com domain).

Additional Notes/Materials

- Add anything else that may be helpful in developing a successful brand name.
- List and/or link to any additional background materials or content to review.

About the Author

Rob Meyerson is the principal and founder of Heirloom, an independent brand strategy and identity firm. He is also the creator and host of the podcast and blog *How Brands Are Built*, on which he has interviewed over three dozen branding and naming experts, including David Aaker, Marty Neumeier, Laura Ries, and Denise Lee Yohn. Prior to Heirloom, Rob's previous roles included head of brand architecture and naming at HP, director of verbal identity at Interbrand in San Francisco, and director of strategy at FutureBrand in Southeast Asia. He has done naming work at three global branding firms, a B2B branding agency, a China-based agency, as head of naming at a Fortune 500 company (HP), and as an independent consultant, for projects in the United States, China, Southeast Asia, and Europe. Rob has written about brand strategy and brand naming for leading publications such as *Entrepreneur, Business Insider, The Guardian,* and *TechCrunch.* He lives in Pacifica, California, with his wife and two children.

Website: robmeyerson.com
Twitter: @RobMeyerson

Index

OTHER TITLES IN THE MARKETING COLLECTION

Naresh Malhotra, Georgia Tech, Editor

- *Fast Fulfillment* by Sanchoy Das
- *Multiply Your Business Value Through Brand & AI* by Rajan Narayan
- *Branding & AI* by Chahat Aggarwal
- *The Business Design Cube* by Rajagopal
- *Customer Relationship Management* by Michael Pearce
- *Stand Out!* by Brian McGurk
- *The Coming Age of Robots* by George Pettinico and George R. Milne
- *Market Entropy* by Rajagopal Rajagopal
- *Decoding Customer Value at the Bottom of the Pyramid* by Ritu Srivastava
- *Qualitative Marketing Research* by Rajagopal

Concise and Applied Business Books

The Collection listed above is one of 30 business subject collections that Business Expert Press has grown to make BEP a premiere publisher of print and digital books. Our concise and applied books are for...

- Professionals and Practitioners
- Faculty who adopt our books for courses
- Librarians who know that BEP's Digital Libraries are a unique way to offer students ebooks to download, not restricted with any digital rights management
- Executive Training Course Leaders
- Business Seminar Organizers

Business Expert Press books are for anyone who needs to dig deeper on business ideas, goals, and solutions to everyday problems. Whether one print book, one ebook, or buying a digital library of 110 ebooks, we remain the affordable and smart way to be business smart. For more information, please visit www.businessexpertpress.com, or contact sales@businessexpertpress.com.

Printed in the USA
CPSIA information can be obtained
at www.ICGtesting.com
LVHW010044080224
771186LV00004B/127